Good
SCOTTISH
GARDENS
GUIDE

Good SCOTTISH GARDENS GUIDE

Joyce and Maurice Lindsay

Chambers

CHAMBERS
An imprint of Larousse plc
43–45 Annandale Street
Edinburgh EH7 4AZ

This edition first published by Chambers 1995

A proportion of the material first published as a Mini Guide by
Chambers 1994

10 9 8 7 6 5 4 3 2 1

A CIP catalogue record for this book is available from
the British Library

ISBN 0 550 22104 2

Illustrations by George Kilgour
Copyright © Larousse plc

Photographs by the National Trust for Scotland, except for those of
Dawyck, Logan and Younger Botanic Gardens, and that of the Royal
Botanic Garden Edinburgh (all by courtesy of the Royal Botanic
Garden Edinburgh).
Copyright © National Trust for Scotland
Copyright © Royal Botanic Garden Edinburgh

Cover photograph of Cawdor Castle
Copyright © Still Moving Picture Co, Edinburgh

Typeset by Pillans & Wilson Ltd,
Edinburgh, Glasgow, London and Manchester
Printed in Great Britain by Clays Ltd, St Ives plc

Alphabetical List of Gardens

Gardens by Areas

Highlands and Islands

Achamore Gardens
Achnacloich
An Cala
Ardanaiseig
Ardchattan Priory
Ardtornish
Arduaine
Balmoral Castle
Barguillean
Brodick Castle Gardens,
  Arran

Bught Floral Hall
Cawdor Castle
Crarae Gardens
Dunrobin Castle
Inverary Castle
Inverewe Gardens
Kilmory Castle
Stonefield Castle Hotel
Torosay Castle, Mull

North-East Scotland

Brechin Castle
Crathes Castle
Drum Castle

Edzell Castle
Kildrummy Castle
Pitmedden

Central Scotland

Bell's Cherrybank Garden
Blairhoyle
Branklyn
Cambo House
Carnell
Cluny House
Colzium-Lennox Estate
  Arboretum and
  Walled Garden
Culzean Castle
Drummond Castle
Earlshall
Falkland Palace
Finlaystone House
Geilston House
Glasgow Botanic Garden
Glenarn
Greenbank Gardens and
  Advice Centre

Hill of Tarvit
Inveresk Lodge
Jane Welsh Carlyle House
  Garden
Kellie Castle
Kinross
Malleny Garden
Pollok House
Royal Botanic Garden
  Edinburgh
St Andrews Botanic Garden
St Mary's Pleasance
Scone Palace
Sir Douglas Bader Garden
  for the Disabled
Strone
Younger Botanic Garden

South-West Scotland

Arbigland
Ardwell House
Bargany
Broughton House
Glenwhan Garden
Lochinch and Castle
  Kennedy
Logan Botanic Garden
Threave School of
  Gardening

South-East Scotland

Abbotsford
Dawyck Botanic Garden
Floors Castle
Kailzie
Little Sparta
Manderston
Mellerstain
Monteviot
Priorwood

This is a *rough* guide to gardens by areas, though it could be argued that Brodick Castle is in Central Scotland, Cawdor and Dunrobin Castle in the North-East, and so on. The intending visitor is advised to refer to his or her map.

Alphabetical List of Colour Plates

For People Who Make Gardens

Snowdrops and crocuses, the spears of Spring,
and daffodils that trumpet brazen measures
in sheeted woodland gardens, laid to bring
from laboured love such wonderment of pleasures.
Flowers in due season, flourishing delight,
quicken surprise. Our troubled senses chime
in grateful peace that brevity unites,
high summer holding back the breath of time.
But Autumn crinkles leaves cloudy with frost;
brown stems collapse; crows in the fringing trees
gargle alarm from thinning branches, tossed
by equinoctial gales that shake and seize
the fade of sappled dankness back to earth;
what gardeners shape again for Spring's next birth.

Maurice Lindsay 30 September 1993

Introduction

Of all the arts man has contrived for his delight, the creation of gardens is one of the most transitory. A fierce attack by weather, pest or disease; neglect resulting from the distractions of war; disinterested titular inheritance, or even a shift of fashion, can quickly result in the destruction of once fine gardens.

In the pages that follow, we have tried to include gardens of every kind, size, taste and fashion: official Botanic gardens, formal gardens ranging from the miniature treasure which is the Pleasance at Edzell Castle to the larger-scale formalities of Pitmedden and Drummond Castle; woodland gardens like Cluny and Crarae, as well as smaller gardens such as Branklyn. We have also included several West Highland gardens, where the astonishing feature, perhaps, is not so much that seasonally they are superb, but that in such prevailing weather and soil conditions it proved possible to create gardens at all. Many such gardens are still in private hands, though others are in the expert care of the National Trust for Scotland.

We have arranged the gardens alphabetically, but provided a listing by geographical division — in view of boundary changes, past and future — and not by Local Authority areas, to enable those travelling in the Borders and the South-East, the South-West, Central Scotland, the North-East and the Highlands and Islands easily to identify the garden delights available in whatever airt they happen to be. While the majority of gardens visited are open to the public with varying degrees of regular frequency, a few are open only on specific days under Scotland's Garden Scheme, from which the entrance fee goes to charity. However, most, if not all, of the owners are willing to allow visits by private arrangement. The days and hours of opening of each garden are indicated at the top of its entry in this book, and visits by private arrangement only are also specified; such limitations should obviously be observed. *The Gardens of Scotland*, published annually, gives the dates of single-day openings in any given year.

We should like to acknowledge the guidance afforded us by the excellent detailed handbooks issued by the National Trust for Scotland for each of the gardens they own and administer, and the guide-books, leaflets and personal information provided by many private owners while we were on our pleasurable tours. Our neighbour and friend, Mrs Fran Walker, also provided us with invaluable source material. Mr and Mrs Robin Hunter afforded us the hospitality of their Border cottage while taking us round some of the gardens in the area.

The Scottish Garden

The Romans are usually credited with introducing horticulture to Britain. While this may have been so in England, in Scotland it seems doubtful if they would have had much opportunity to carry out such peaceful pursuits while manning the Antonine Wall.

It seems more probable that the first gardens to be cultivated in Scotland were associated with the early Christian settlements, whose nuns and monks grew herbs and flowers for medicinal or culinary purposes. There is an 18th-century reference suggesting that traces of gardening near Iona Abbey could still be seen at that time. The great Abbey of Melrose was once famous for its monastic orchards. In the garden at Prior-wood, immediately adjacent, this tradition is being carried on today with the planting of some of the older and rarer varieties of apple tree. David I is said to have created a garden at the foot of Edinburgh Castle. In his *Caledonia Depicta,* George Chalmers, writing in 1907, asserts that the Scottish nobles began to follow David's example on their own estates.

After the Reformation, from about 1560, the lands of the religious houses were either sold off or gifted to men who formed a new landed class. Following the Union of the Crowns in 1603, there was no longer any need for Scottish houses to be defensive. An example of this more relaxed graciousness was King James VI's Knot Garden, beneath Stirling Castle, the grassed-over mounds of which may still be seen today. It was probably laid out about 1625 by one William Watts, and 'consisted of two adjacent gardens whose geometrical pattern of clipped box hedges were punctuated by ornamental trees standing like soldiers', as Tim Buxbaum puts it in his *Scottish Garden Building: from Food to Folly* (1989). We know that Watts was paid for 'plotting and contryveing his Majestie's new orchard and garden'. The garden at Edzell, now restored and replanted, had been laid out in 1604 by the Lindsays. The great formal garden at Pitmedden, now brilliantly restored, has the largest surviving parterre in Scotland. It was laid out about 1675 by Alexander Seton.

The country house and its working estate quickly became the centre of the local economy, its agricultural efficiency providing the money for such leisure pursuits as garden-making. The medieval run-rig system of cultivating unfence strips increasingly gave way to enclosure, the creation fields. By the beginning of the 18th century, too, there w dearth of trees; therefore tree-planting was carried ou considerable scale. In 1729, William Mackintosh of published *An Essay On Ways and Means for Inclosing, Planting etc. Scotland*. Adam Cockburn of Ormiston was pioneering agricultural improvements in the Lothians. There was nation-wide support for The Society of Improvers of the Knowledge of Agriculture in Scotland, formed in Edinburgh in 1729, with the Dukes of Atholl, Hamilton and Perth, and the Earls of Haddington, Stair and Wemyss among its patrons.

The initial impulse to create pleasure-gardens was inspired by the examples of classical antiquity and of Renaissance Europe. The Emperor Hadrian was said to have laid out for himself such a garden, as did Pope Julius, and later, Cardinal d'Este, at the Vatican and Tivoli. These early gardens were very much status symbols, one of the reasons why, in a different form, they were thought worth emulating down the centuries. They were also manifestations of orderly arrangement as well as of grandeur. Further inspiration came from the gardens André Le Nôtre designed in France at Vaux-le-Vicomte (1660) for the financier Fouquet and at Versailles for the king himself.

The medieval interest in herb and fruit-growing probably played some part in the Scots tradition of mixing the plants of necessity, so to speak, with those grown purely for aesthetic satisfaction. In pre-Reformation days most of the orchard trees probably came from France, but not everything from more hospitable climes could adapt to the inclement weather and the limitations of the soil in some parts of the country. The first book deliberately to take account of such matters was *The Scots Gardener* (or *Gard'ner*, as it was printed on the title page of the first edition of 1683) by John Reid.

Reid was gardener to Sir George Mackenzie of Rosehaugh, who lived at Avoch, Rosshire. To the Covenanters, whom he persecuted for treason in the king's name, he was 'Bluidy Mackenzie'. He was also Lord Advocate, an early agricultural improver, strong defender of what he called 'the *Scottish* idiom of the *British* tongue', founder of the Advocates' Library in Edinburgh and author of what is generally regarded as the first Scottish novel, *Aretina* (1606). Reid's book falls into two parts. In the first, he deals with layout and construction, what he describes as 'contriving and planting gardens, orchards, avenues, groves, with new and profitable wayes of levelling; and how to measure and divide land'.

Reid was a great believer in symmetry, telling us: 'In a confined situation of ground, I add what I can but diminish nothing. I take a survey of the work and when I find several gular and irregular things done on one side of the house, nothing correspondent on the other, I work the very same e opposite side, and this I continue to do till two arities produce one uniformity.'

Incidentally, he gave sound advice on making a lawn: 'To lay grass, first level the ground, whether a walk or a plot; and 'tis better to lye a year so made up, before you lay the turf; because it may be levelled up again, if it sink with holes; if it lye wet, bottom it with stones and rubbish; and if the earth be fat, take it out and put in sand . . . Let the turf be of equal thickness, near inch and a half thick, a foot and a half broad, and as much in length; lay their green sides together when you put them in the cart, but do not roll them when brought home. Lay them all even and close, feeling each particular turf with your foot, so as you may discern any inequality, to be helped immediately.' He was good, too, on pruning: 'Begin betimes to prune your fruit-trees; spare them not while young; reduce them into good shape and order while such, so they will not only overgrow their wounds, their branches being but small, but also, when they should come to bear fruit, you shall not need to cut so much, only purge them of superfluities, and this is the way to make trees fruitful as well as pleasant.'

There was a different view on how to create an expansive impression in a garden other than by formal symmetry. This was exemplified by the garden that the patriot opponent of incorporating Union, Andrew Fletcher, designed for his garden at Saltoun. He favoured a series of rectangular enclosures without any 'symmetry or correspondence of parts', unity being achieved by connecting the feature-points in his layouts with a series of sight-lines. Where walls interfered with the 'lines', he constructed see-through points, or, as the French would call them, *clairvoyées*.

Sir William Bruce, the first great Scottish architect, was also a layer-out of gardens. He favoured Reid's balancing when it came to buildings, but used the 'sight-line' when designing his gardens. At his own house of Balcaskie in Fife, he used the distant (and sometimes haar-obscured) Bass Rock as the centre 'line', on either side of which his 'regularity' allowed for a variety of plot-shapes and plantings; at Kinross, he lined up on the ruin of Loch Leven Castle, in the middle of the loch. At Hopetoun, he used North Berwick Law. This 'termination' idea, as it was sometimes called, was also employed by 'Bobbing John', the 11th Earl of Mar—he who led the unsuccessful Jacobite Rising of 1715—on the grandest scale at Alloa, Clackmannanshire. He laid out his garden between 1706 and 1714, using, in the words of John Macky in *A Journey Through Scotland in Familiar Letters from a Gentleman Here to his Friends Abroad* (1729), '32 different vistas, each ending on some remarkable seat or mountain at some miles distant', one being Stirling Castle; another the Palace of Elphinstone; third the Castle of Clacmanning (Clackmannan). Lack means and then the exile which followed the Earl's Jacobite adventure meant that his 'grand design' was never fully realized.

The gathering pace of agricultural improvement in the second half of the 18th century contributed towards the move away from the formal garden, which was expensive in manpower at a time when increasingly agriculture was demanding more labour.

William Adam, though primarily an architect, also prepared garden designs where required, expanding on Bruce's ideas at Hopetoun. His contemporary, William Boutcher, a nurseryman, likewise went in for garden design. The two of them were employed by the remarkable Sir John Clerk of Penicuik—composer, poet, gardener, amateur architect, Baron of Exchequer and Commissioner for the Union—at his 'villa' of Mavisbank in Midlothian, subsequently undermined by coal mines and internally half-destroyed by fire in the 20th century, but, as one of William Adam's masterpieces, recently acquired by the Secretary of State for Scotland for restoration. At Hurley Pond, on Sir John's Penicuik estate, he experimented with the kind of landscape gardening being cultivated by Launcelot ('Capability') Brown, and to some extent by his Scottish followers, although the flat English countryside probably lent itself more readily to landscape treatment than the Scottish terrain, with its more varied natural features.

Henry Home, Lord Kames, included a section on gardening in his once-influential *Elements of Criticism*, published in 1763. Kames favoured judicious planting emphasizing whatever quality each portion of a garden might possess. Thus 'a rocky crag edging a gully would demand Scots pines and ruined buildings', or a folly. A gloomy place would suggest yews and so on. 'Planting and layout', he felt, 'should be arranged to rouse as many different emotions as possible, though preserving harmony. For that reason, a ruin, affording a sort of melancholy pleasure, ought not to be seen from a flower-parterre, which is gay and cheerful. But to pass immediately from an exhilarating object to a ruin, has a glorious effect.'

The real father of the great Victorian garden was possibly J C Loudon. He invented the word 'Gardenesque' to describe the planting of trees and shrubs for their botanical qualities, the plants being treated both as specimens and as ornaments in themselves. For that effect to succeed, however, the range of available plants had to be extended.

It is unlikely that extensive flower-planting in Scotland would have been widely practised before the foundation of the Botanic Garden in Edinburgh in 1670 by Sir Robert Sibbald, author of *Scotia Illustrata*. At Taymouth about this time, we know that the Earl of Breadalbane had honeysuckle, laburnum and roses, then relatively new. Older-established plants included violets, mandrakes, poppies, cornflowers, foxgloves, daffodils and gentians. Reid's book of 1683 describes a garden using crocuses, anemones, cowslips, gillyflowers, carnations and tulips, while Sir William Bruce used narcissus, lilies, hyacinths and double jonquils, all imported from Europe. By 1789, Lady Bute had zinnias and campanulas, as well as dahlias. Also by that time, botanists had become curious about species from further afield, and widening trade made voyages of horticultural exploration more of an economic possibility.

During the late 18th century, throughout the 19th, and well into the 20th, the range of plants available to gardeners was constantly being extended, as the result of the discoveries of a number of distinguished plant collectors, many of them Scots. These men made difficult, often dangerous, journeys into distant and little-explored places in search of plants and seeds. There were, of course, enthusiastic amateurs like Burns's friend and correspondent, John Arnot of Dalquhatswood, near Galston. At one time he was involved in trading, both in the East Indies and China, and plants and seeds were brought back from these expeditions. Writing from Dalquhatswood to Lord Loudon in October 1769 after one such journey, he sent his lordship 'a pott containing the stones of the fruit called Leechee' and 'a book of Chinese paintings'. No doubt John Arnot of Dalquhatswood was but one of many such collectors.

The first great professional Scottish collector, however, was a young Aberdonian, Francis Masson (1741–1805), who had for several years been gardening at Kew. He went out to South Africa in 1772, aboard a ship whose master was Captain Cook. The expedition was planned by Joseph (later Sir Joseph) Banks (1743–1820), who had himself sailed as the naturalist with Cook on his first voyage of exploration. Soon, plants from Masson were being shipped back to Kew, though many died on the long voyage home. Seeds therefore became the preferred method of importation. Joining forces with the Swedish Carl Thunberg—a pupil of Linnaeus (1707–78), who devised the universal Latin system of naming plants—from the area between the Cape and Karoo Masson collected Cape Heaths (over 100 varieties), ixias, lachenalias, gazanias, mesembryanthemums and the white arum lily, *Zantedeschia aethiopica*. On a subsequent trip, he found the Guernsey lily, *Nerine sarniensis*, a mis-reference since its original habitat was not the Channel Islands but Table Mountain, above Cape Town. Legend has it that some bulbs washed ashore from a wreck off Guernsey were planted and flowered; hence the name.

Other trips followed—to the Karoo again, the Canaries, the Azores, the West Indies, then back to the Cape, where near Cape Town Masson eventually set up a small nursery. After being nearly drowned in 1779 when his ship was attacked by the French, Masson again visited Canada, *Trillium grandiflorum* resulting from that trip.

Twenty years after Masson's death, a Forfar nurseryman, Thomas Drummond (1790–1837) sailed as assistant naturalist on Sir John Franklin's second Arctic expedition. Despatched to the Rocky Mountains, Drummond spent an incredibly arduous year—at one point coming near to starvation—collecting plants, mainly for study purposes. At least one garden plant, *Dryas drummondii*, commemorates his name. He then accompanied one of the most famous of all plant collectors, David Douglas (1799–1834), a young Scone gardener who trained at the Palace and at Valleyfield, near Culross. In 1820, Douglas moved to Glasgow's Botanic Garden, where he attended Dr William Hooker's lectures (Hooker later became Director at Kew); Douglas subsequently made a short trip to New York, which resulted in the collection of some fruit trees. On his second trip, he teamed up with Drummond.

Douglas went to North America via Cape Horn and the Galapagos Islands, arriving on the western coast of North America in 1825. His 'haul' this time included the flowering currant, *Ribes sanguineum*; the bramble, *Rubus spectabilis*; the ground-coverer (now almost a weed), *Gaultheria shallon*; the Californian poppy, *Eschscholtzia californica*, lupins, penstemons and the Monkey flower, *Mimulus moschatus*. Above all, he collected conifer seeds in such profusion that he joked with Hooker, 'You will begin to think that I manufacture pines at my pleasure.' Today, the best-known of the conifers bears his name, the Douglas Fir.

In 1829, another visit to North America produced a red larkspur, *Delphinium cardinale*, and also *Limnanthes douglasii* and *Garrya elliptica*, a catkin-bearing shrub, among many others. He also made several visits to Hawaii, where Captain Cook was murdered. The 35-year-old Douglas was apparently inspecting the edge of a pit in which a bullock had been trapped for food, when the edge of the pit gave way. Douglas fell in and tragically was trampled to death. A memorial in his honour was put up at Scone in 1841.

John Fraser (1750–1811) collected in the eastern half of North America, finding *Uvularia grandiflora*. John Lyon (c.1770) was responsible for the discovery of *Iris fulva, Dicentra eximia* and *Pieris floribunda*. Their contemporary, James Main (1775–1846), collected in China in 1792. En route he stopped off in Cape Town, where he met Masson and saw his nursery. Main brought back (mostly purchased from Cantonese nurseries) camellias, Tree paeonies, *Spiraea crenata* and *Chaenomeles speciosa*, among many other specimens.

Following the 1840 opium war and the Treaty of Nanking in 1842, Britain gained Hong Kong and better trading conditions in mainland China. As a result, the London Horticultural Society sent out Robert Fortune (1813–80) in 1843. He was born at Chirnside, Berwickshire, and trained in the gardens of nearby Kelloe House. In 1839, he went to the Royal Botanic Garden Edinburgh, serving under William McNab, who recommended him to the Chiswick Garden of the London Horticultural Society (not 'Royal', incidentally, until 1861). Fortune's mission was to collect tea plants for cultivation in India. Dressed as a Chinaman, he travelled inland (at some risk, becoming involved in several hair-raising adventures). Eventually he returned home with chrysanthemums, azaleas, Tree paeonies, the Japanese anemone, camellias, the Winter jasmine, the Chinese Snowball tree, diervilla, *Weigela florida*, and a plant soon to become enormously popular in Victorian gardens, 'Bleeding Heart'. Later trips to China and Japan produced *Lilium auratum*, *Clematis lanuginosa* and the rhododendron named after him, *R fortunei*.

China was again plant-hunted by Falkirk-born George Forrest (1873–1937) early in the 20th century. After spending some time in Australia, he joined the Royal Botanic Garden Edinburgh, and was sent by private patronage to Yunnan. He was ambushed by a gang of Tibetans when at Tseku. From a party of 80, he was one of only 14 to escape alive. Forrest was to be responsible for bringing to Britain hundreds of new rhododendrons and primulas, the gentian, *Gentiana sino-ornata*, and several Blue poppies, many lilies and a large collection of dwarf plants and alpines. The dwarf *Rhododendron forrestii* bears his name, although he introduced many other varieties, including the tall *R protistum*, and more than 300 others.

During the Twenties and Thirties of the present century, George Sherriff (1898–1967) and his friend Frank Ludlow (1895–1972) made several expeditions to south-east Tibet and Kashmir. In 1938 they were accompanied by George Taylor (later Sir George), the then Director of the Royal Botanic Gardens at Kew. Ludlow and Sherriff made a final expedition in 1949–50. Sherriff retired to Ascreavie, near Kirriemuir, where he died in 1967. His widow, Betty, who had accompanied her husband on his last two expeditions, thereafter tended his garden with skilful care until her own death in 1978.

The formal gardens of earlier times gave place in the 19th century to wooded gardens or planted parkland, usually with walled garden. This, however, was now located at some distance from the house, so that the occupants, as one writer put it, 'would not be distressed by cartloads of dung'. Georgian houses were often either ruthlessly replaced or extended as the wealth of Empire poured into Britain in its Land-of-Hope-and-Glory heyday. The opulent Victorian and Edwardian country house life-style necessitated the employment of many gardeners, but both money and self-confidence began to falter in the wake of World War I. There was a further falling away after 1946, when country houses and their gardens disappeared in huge numbers. Today, even in maintained woodland gardens, many once-brilliant walled gardens shelter only weeds.

A distinguished restoring architect who also took thoughtful account of the value and placing of gardens was Robert (later Sir Robert) Lorimer (1864–1929). His former home, the restored Kellie Castle, is only one of his many Scottish achievements. Early in his career, he wrote:

'To me as an architect, the interesting thing about the house is that the plan has not been interfered with or modernised, and the exterior of the house is practically untouched. So many of the fine old Scottish houses were ruined by Bryce and others fifty or sixty years ago, the old portion being entirely surrounded by modern work; whereas, when it is necessary to add to an old Scotch house, the old portion ought to be allowed to stand up and tell its own story, and the new portion should be joined on to it by some narrow neck so that there can be no question as to which is old and which is new.

'One of the characteristics of Kellie is the fact that the walled garden enters directly out of the house, and that the flowers and fruit, and vegetables are all mixed up together . . .

'I always think the ideal plan is to have the park, with the sheep or beasts grazing in it, coming right under the windows at one side of the house and the gardens attached to the house at the other side. We could not quite manage this at Kellie, but put as light a fence as possible between the lawn and the park.'

Kellie, like Crathes and Pitmedden in Aberdeenshire and Branklyn in Perth, is fortunate in that it is now in the care of the National Trust for Scotland, whose integrity in adhering, wherever possible, to the original design of a garden is matched with the highest standard of horticultural skills.

Some country houses have become hotels and their ounds have been maintained. The future of walled gardens in privately owned country houses, however, does not, on the whole, look hopeful. Let us enjoy those that remain while they still survive.

In these pages we have chronicled the results of our visits to several private gardens at a time when some of their owners are obviously finding it difficult to maintain standards; yet all have something to offer, making a visit worthwhile. We delighted in the West Highland gardens, some clearly struggling to hold back the ever-encroaching thrust of exuberant nature; others, like Ardchattan Priory (the ruins of which are cared for by Historic Scotland, itself now in the garden-preserving business), achieving considerable success, with the added bonus of being set in spectacular scenery.

There is also good news of re-creations and even creation. A new Walled Garden will shortly be embarked upon at Tower of Lethendy, near Blairgowrie. In the North-East, Dorothy and Willy Newlands, who have had Ian Begg carry out one of his 'creative restorations' on Lauriston Castle, are in the process of restoring the garden, while near Hamilton, Bill and Sandra Fleming intend to restore the terraced gardens, perched high above the Avon at Barncluith House, first created in 1583 by John Hamilton, to their former glory.

We have seen every garden described in this book. While gardens can deteriorate with alarming speed, we feel confident that those who do visit the gardens of our choice will not come away without having shared our satisfaction and delight.

ABBOTSFORD

Owner: Mrs Patricia Maxwell-Scott, OBE

Off A7, 2 miles from Melrose and a similar distance from Galashiels

Daily from 3rd Monday in March to 31 October from 1000 hours to 1700 hours
Sundays from 1400 hours to 1700 hours

The home of Sir Walter Scott is of world-wide interest because of the extraordinary influence the Waverley Novels had on the burgeoning European Romantic Movement. It must always be of special interest to Scots, since those of the novels which deal with the historical crisis-points of Scotland's history made Scots readers for the first time aware of their past, the documents previously perused by scholars being inaccessible to the general reader.

Sir Walter bought the farm of Cartley Hole (also known as Clarty Hole), together with about 100 surrounding acres, in 1811, buying an adjacent tract up to Cauldshields Loch in 1813. In 1817, he made his largest purchase, the lands of Toftfield. Cartley Hole reputedly contained a former haunt of Thomas the Rhymer. It also commanded a magnificent view across the Tweed. The name, Abbotsford, was chosen by Scott after a ford over which the monks of Melrose once drove their cattle.

Scott first built a cottage on the estate, to which he moved from his rented home, Ashiesteel, in 1813. The mansion itself was built between 1817 and 1821, largely to his own design and incorporating historical fragments or copies, such as a gateway from Linlithgow, a portal from Edinburgh's Old Tolbooth and a roof from Roslin Chapel. Its external miscellany of gables, projecting windows, hanging turrets and surmounting towers may indeed seem an architect's nightmare; yet it is oddly beautiful, 'a romance in stone and lime' as it has been called or, in Scott's own words, 'a place to dream of, not to tell.'

Sir Walter himself first laid out both the grounds and the garden. The entrance drive leads through the ~tural garden with its viburnums, dogwoods, shrub

12

roses, azaleas, rhododendrons and potentillas, interspersed with yews, conifers, silver birch and rowans.

The South Court garden (the walls of which were built by the Smiths of Darnick, who also extended the house itself) has a yew hedge on the south wall planted by Mr J Hope-Scott in the 1860s, replacing Scott's pergola of roses. (An example of ecological economy is practised in that the yew clippings eventually go to Germany where they are used in cancer research). Spaces have been cut to show five medallions from the old Edinburgh Mercat (market) Cross, pulled down in 1756 and presented to Scott by Sir Henry Raeburn. From the Tolbooth, too, comes the bowl of the fountain in the centre which in 1660 ran with wine for the people on the Restoration of Charles II. There are also rectangular stones from the Roman Camp at Old Penrith and part of an inscription of the 22nd Legion. Linking the South Court to the East Court is a screen copied from the Cloisters at Melrose Abbey. At its feet, there is a border of pink roses and violet violas. In the East Court there is Sir Walter's sundial, as well as John Greenshield's statue of Morris (the exciseman in *Rob Roy*) pleading for mercy from Helen Macgregor, presented to Abbotsford after Scott's death. At the far end, roses and clematis clamber up the walls behind a border of paeonies. Immaculately trimmed conical yews are placed symmetrically in both Court gardens.

A clematis and an apple tree overhang the entrance into the Walled Garden itself, where, after the old Scots fashion, there are to be found flowers, fruit and vegetables. Two herbaceous borders slope up gently to the Orangerie, for the original construction of which Sir Walter was responsible and which dominates this main axis of the garden. He also had hot pipes fitted into the garden wall for his fruit, after the Roman fashion.

In the upper border there is a lovely example of the old hybrid rugosa, *Rosa* 'Blanc Double de Coubert', which is matched in the lower border by an equally fragrant *R* 'Roserai de L'Hay'. Roses, indeed, are a feature at Abbotsford.

The two herbaceous borders contain both the customary perennials as well as annuals for later summer colour. These include purple heliotrope, cosmos, nicotiana and superb blood-red dahlias. Other box-edged beds contain decorative, but also culinarily delicious, Globe artichokes, sweetpeas, chrysanthemums, white anaphalis, fuchsias and lily of the valley. The flowers from Abbotsford are frequently in demand for local functions, as one might expect.

It is a garden of considerable charm, to some extent inevitably overshadowed by the scenic setting and, of course, the influence of the house itself.

Clematis montana

ACHAMORE GARDENS, Isle of Gigha

Owner: Mr Derek Holt of Holt Leisure Parks; gardens under the protection and guidance of the National Trust for Scotland, who own the plants

Off A83 Lochgilphead to Campbeltown road at Tayinloan from where the ferry leaves

Daily almost all year round

The island of Gigha (or the 'Isle of God') lies a brief ferry journey across the sound of the same name from Tayinloan on Kintyre's west coast. It is miniature in size, being a mere 6 miles long by 1½ miles wide, but it contains a wide variety of flora and fauna, thanks to the mildness of the climate and the variation of the terrain. Washed by the Gulf Stream, the island rejoices in its warmth and therefore rarely suffers from severe frosts. The salt-laden Atlantic gales, however, do batter it, but at the southern end, where Achamore Gardens are situated, a carefully positioned barrier of sycamore and spruce, planted at the turn of the century as cover for game, now protects this fine garden, as do the other shelter belts planted strategically throughout the policies in similar fashion to those at Inverewe. Another form of protection from the fierce winds is provided by *Rhododendron ponticum*, now becoming a curse in certain areas of the Highlands, though its rampant canopy is welcome on Gigha.

The Achamore Gardens were created by Lt-Colonel Sir James Horlick Bart when he bought the island in 1944. On his death, they were presented to the National Trust for Scotland along with an endowment which formed the Horlick Garden Fund, its object being the propagation and dispersal of the garden's many rarities among others of the Trust's properties. A keen and expert gardener, Sir James's chief interest lay in breeding and propagating rhododendrons which thrive in the peaty soil here, as they do in so many Scottish west-coast gardens. His famous crosses are firmly established at Achamore along with a wide variety of species and hybrids brought from abroad. Gardeners are usually generous with their gifts and Horlic rhododendrons can be seen at Brodick Castle (wh the Trust is carrying out an ambitious programme propagation) and Strone in Argyll. It was a two-way traffic. Southern beeches, *Nothofagus*, and *Pinus leucodermis*, the Bosnian pine, were established at Achamore having been gifted by the Campbells of Crarae on Loch Fyne.

The Gardens embrace 50 acres through which 2½ miles of winding paths lead the visitor ever onward. Here there is that shelter in which the more tender species such as embothriums, camellias, and the large collection of plants from Chile, the Antipodes, Japan and China, revel. There are cherries from Japan, Australian pittosporums, New Zealand flax, *Phormium tenax*, *Eucryphia glutinosa* and *Lomatia ferruginea* from Chile, American rowans, our own native birches; the collection is, indeed, international.

Perfume is indispensable in a real garden. So many of our modern roses are perfect in shape, colour and form but frequently lack scent. In Achamore the old rugosa rose, 'Roseraie de L'Hay' and its hybrid 'Blanc Double de Coubert' perfume the evening air. The early *Hamamelis mollis*, Chinese Witch Hazel, with its curious yellow spidery petals, also adds to the garden's fragrance, as do the many lilies and rhododendrons like *R polyanthemum*, one of the best. An evergreen *Atherosperma moschatum* from Australia also contributes its perfume.

In front of the Scottish baronial-style house, finished in 1884 and designed by Glasgow architect John Honeyman, a gently sloping bank provides an ideal habitat for a great spread of daffodils, while the sides of the winding paths through the estate are carpeted by more daffodils. In spring, sheets of snowdrops light up the short days. To the east of the house, ericas and callunas add colour to a border containing hardy perennials like geraniums (not pelargoniums), primulas and aquilegias.

No west-coast Scottish garden would be complete without the azaleas. Here, they and diverse rhododendrons in profusion are the glory of Achamore. In the cabeanum Wood, as one would expect, are located larger-leafed specimens, including that giving its name to this particular area. The collection is of world-wide renown. You will find some of these lovely bushes flowering as early as March. There are small-leaved ones like 'Blue Tit', 'Humming-Bird' and 'Elizabeth' and also the gigantic leaved *sinogrande*, plus the magnificent *falconeri*. The variety is almost endless.

As if that were not enough, there are the camellias such as 'Donation', 'Citation', 'Inspiration' — the catalogue of names reads like a litany; a Hospital Garden (the name is a misnomer for there are no sick plants here); a Pond Garden containing hostas, gunnera (named after a Norwegian botanist), astilbes and primulas, each species flourishing against a background of grey *Leptospermum pubescens*. There are other gardens, two of them walled.

Mention must be made of the magnificent trees. These include the rare *Abies Kawakamii* from Formosa and others of the same family. Betulas and two Coffin junipers, *Jun recurva coxii*, thujas, a Turkey Oak, *Quercus cerris*, a Norway Maple, *Acer platanoides*, amongst many others, contribute shape, height, colour and texture of foliage throughout the year.

Visitors to these remarkable gardens have two choices — a shorter walk following blue arrows takes about half an hour during which many of the delights can be inspected. Those of a more robust constitution can follow the green arrows on a route taking about two hours. Having revelled in the marvels of Achamore, the envious (and there will be many) may purchase plants from the Boat House, or by mail order.

Achamore Gardens provide a congenial habitat for a host of different birds as do the cliffs on the west coast of the island for the many gulls and other sea-birds.

Those interested in wild flowers will find a visit to Gigha a very rewarding experience as the differing habitats nurture a large variety of plantlife.

As an unexpected, but probably rather rare, bonus on a clear day (a very clear day, no doubt) we are told the coast of Labrador, lying due west, can be seen, presumably by the very keen-sighted. We did not see it

ACHNACLOICH, Connel

Owner: Mrs J Nelson

3 miles east of Connel off the A85

5 April to 11 June, and early August to the end of October, from 1000 hours to 1800 hours

Achnacloich is a grandiose, castellated mansion by John Starforth of Glasgow, standing on a promontory on the south side of Loch Etive. Its garden was first laid out in Victorian and Edwardian times, when the terraces, the walled garden (now mainly growing fruit and vege- tables) and the walled look-outs, with strategically placed seats for the enjoyment of the magnificent views above Loch Etive, were constructed. Very soon after the house was erected the large Douglas fir beside it was planted.

Between the two World Wars, many species of rhododendrons were established, those of the triflo- rum varieties having seeded themselves with ease. Banks of azaleas beside the approach drive to the house were also planted in the 1930s, as well as Japanese maple, *Enkianthus campanulatus, E perulatus* and clumps of berberis, which provide splendid autumn colouring.

In the 1950s, dense masses of the ubiquitous *Rhododendron ponticum* were cleared away by the then proprietor, Mr T E Nelson, a distinguished plantsman, leaving a canopy of oak, some of it descended from the ancient trees of the Caledonian Forest. These are interspersed with some fine speci- mens of European larch and Scots pine, planted in the 1820s. Being relatively frost free, embothriums grow to the height of some of the oaks. In early spring, there is a fine flowering of bulbs; pale daffodils (rather than the brasher bright yellow varieties) light up the lawn and the dells, where there are also carpets of Wind Flowers, *Anemone nemerosa,* wild hyacinths and primroses. In May, *Crinodendron hookerianum* is in full flower, while in summer, various clethras, resplendent specimens of *Eucryphia glutinosa* and *Hoheria lyallii* flourish. Magno- lias are here too—varieties such as *mollicomata, ·bovata, wilsonii, sprengeri diva*—and the more tender

18

rhododendrons of the maddenii series are equally at home. Amidst the little hills and glens that are a feature of the garden are two small pools with Candelabra primulas nearby, rodgersias, irises and other bog-loving plants, including the golden-yellow *Lysichiton*. Beside one of the pools there is a choice Kilmarnock willow (*Salix caprea* 'pendula').

A new development was begun in 1990 in an area east of the house which, suitably cleared, is now planted out with a variety of tender shrubs and beyond — gean, birch, sorbus, willow, eucalyptus and others, numbering 80 species in all.

As with so many Highland gardens, Achnacloich is undoubtedly at its best in spring, and again when in autumn colour. At the season's end there are the heart-shaped leaves of *Cercidiphyllum japonicum*, their springtime purple now turned to a rich scarlet and yellow; the bright red-berried small rowan, *Sorbus vilmorinii*; and the orange-turning leaves of the sorbus 'Joseph Rock'. As autumn rustles in, too, the Enkianthus that flowered in spring turns gold and red as the acer *A pensylvanicum*'s large three-lobed leaves become a rich yellow.

Enkianthus campanulatus

AN CALA, Ellenabeich, Isle of Seil

Owners: Mr and Mrs Thomas Downie

B844, 16 miles south of Oban on the road to Easdale, Isle of Seil

9 March to 30 September
from 1000 hours to 1800 hours

Gardens exposed to the winds on the west coast of Scotland need to be sheltered. The Gaelic name *An cala* means 'the haven' or 'place of peace'. Part of the village of Easdale, once a quarrying island, the garden sits on a horseshoe-shaped coign, sheltered by wooded cliffs on three sides. The conifers planted round it are now higher than the cliffs. The house, once a distillery, was later converted to three cottages, one of which was inherited by Colonel Arthur Murray, later Lord Elibank, from his aunt. He was married to the actress Faith Celli, who took part in many Shaw plays and was a famous Peter Pan in her day. When she heard of her husband's inheritance, she exclaimed, 'Good! Now, I can create a garden!'

After acquiring the other two cottages, that is precisely what they did at considerable cost and effort. As Lord Elibank recalled, 'In 1934, to keep out the west and north-west gales, we built the grey brick wall 15 feet high', red brick being unsuitable for the prevailing slate colour of the island. The Colonel had to dynamite large sections of rock in order to create the garden and imported thousands of tons of topsoil, mainly from Ayrshire.

Several burns run through the garden. The main one was dammed here and there, thus creating ponds at various levels. The sides of the burns were then planted with astilbes, mimulus, a variety of hostas, *Iris kaempferi*, a selection of different primulas, rodgersias, *Filipendula hexapetala*, willows, gentians such as *asclepiadea* and ferns, in accordance with a plan devised by Mrs Murray.

The Lily Pond carries the reflection of a Willow-leaved pear, *Pyrus salcifolia*, and the statue of a stooping water-nymph.

Cherry trees from Japan, fashionable in the 1930s, include two magnificent 'Tai haku' and several 'Oku Myaico', as well as 'Ojochin, Mount Fuji' and 'Jo-nioi'. Azaleas also feature, mostly the rock garden variety. Thymes, gentians, iberis, Rock phloxes and the Alpine willow, *Salix reticulata,* flourish among the rocky outcrops, as well as sedums, sempervivums, Rock roses, aubretias and *Alyssum saxatile*.

Here too are those roses able to withstand the salt winds, notably 'Else Poulsen' and 'Karen Poulsen', both now elderly but still providing a fine show of summer colour. Mrs Downie is currently engaged in replenishing the herbaceous borders. As everywhere else now in the Highlands, ponticum rhododendrons are in evidence along the woodland paths. Seats in various sections of this delightful garden provide breathtaking views of the isles of Scarba, the Garvellachs, Mull and, in the distance, Jura and Luing.

Prunus 'Tai-haku'

ARBIGLAND, Kirkbean

Owner: Captain J B Blackett

14 miles south of Dumfries, signposted from Kirkbean on A710

*April to September daily
from 1000 hours to 1800 hours*

Arbigland, an estate of 1400 acres on the Solway Firth, has been owned down the years by Murray ancestors of the Earls of Mansfield, the Earl of Annandale and, briefly, by the Earl of Southesk, who in 1722 sold it for 22 000 Scots pounds to the rich Craik family, merchants in Dumfries and Cumberland. Prior to the Craik ownership, the area was a windswept peninsula of gorse and rocks. The Craiks were amongst the greatest of the early agricultural improvers.

William Craik, who designed the present house in the style of Adam—the porch is a later addition—in 1755 (when it cost him £4000) was responsible for the walled garden (not open to the public) and probably also for the pond. Craik died, aged 95, in 1798 and was succeeded by his cousin, Douglas Hamilton Craik, who came back from America to take over the lairdship. His son, John, sold the estate in 1852 to an ancestor of the present owner.

There are other American connections. About 1730, William Craik's head gardener was one John Paul, who had learned his craft on an estate outside Edinburgh and who laid out 10 acres of the grounds much as they are today. John Paul and his wife, Jean Duff, lived in a cottage south of the main gates and had several children, one of whom, John, was born in 1747. He became John Paul Jones, one-time buccaneer and later the founding father of the American navy. All Craik's legitimate children predeceased him, but an illegitimate son, James, became a doctor, and emigrated to America, where he became George Washington's medical adviser and lifelong friend. The present main gates, incidentally, were built about 1805 by Allan Cunningham, mason turned poet, still remembered today for his song, *A Wet Sheet and a Flowing Sea*. A spinster daughter, Helen, who died in 1825, was in

Brodick Castle and Garden

page 53

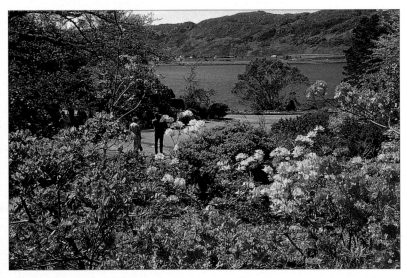

Inverewe Gardens *azaleas*

page 124

Drum Castle *Rose Garden* page 82

Greenbank Gardens *spring bedding* page 115

correspondence with Robert Burns. Two of his letters to her have survived. The poet visited Arbigland. A versifier herself, Helen was the authoress of five anonymous novels.

The real architect of the garden in its present form was Captain Blackett's grandmother, who was widowed in World War I and thereafter settled at Arbigland. Entirely self-taught, she was responsible for the sunken garden, the terraces overlooking the sea, and the heath bank behind the House-on-the-Shore, which she built as a dower house in the 1930s. Captain Beauchamp Blackett came to live in Arbigland in 1970, when the old lady was in her mid-eighties and maintaining the garden was becoming too much for her. She had, however, made an excellent choice of plants to suit the windy, wet but mild climate and the soil—'neutral boulder clay over limestone', but enriched by 'liberal dumpings over the centuries of leafmould and peat', as one commentator put it. She planted a selection of rhododendrons, azaleas, camellias, eucryphias, pieris, ribes and cercis, as well as shrubs that colour up brilliantly in autumn, like *Parrotia persica*, numerous acers, *Cercidiphyllum japonicum* and *Hydrangea villosa*. When she died in 1974, Captain Blackett considered whether simply to forget about the garden, or to restore and maintain it. Happily, he chose the latter course.

The garden is approached by the Broad Walk, constructed about 1680 at the same time as the stable block, which now houses a tearoom. It is a long avenue planted with many rare and magnificent trees, including an *Abies procera* 'Glauca', a *Cedrus deodara* and an *Araucaria araucana*, or Monkey Puzzle.

To the left is the area known as 'Japan', a water garden with many varieties of primulas, hostas and rodgersias. The paths in 'Japan' lead to the pond, beyond which there is a wide selection of shrubs including several types of acer, *Cupressus macrocarpa* 'Lutea', *Itea ilicifolia*, *Fothergilla major* and, tucked away along one of the paths, a fine *Rhododendron sinogrande*. To the left there is a private area and another tree-lined path leading to the scant cliff-top remains of McCulloch's

Castle, an early Gallovidian whose exploits, perhaps fortunately, are not recorded.

Between the pond and the path to the sea shore is the sunken garden, laid out with roses. Here, too, you will find a *Passiflora caerulea* clambering up the surrounding wall with a Jackmanii clematis as a fellow traveller. Tree paeonies, large bushes of *Fuchsia magellanica* and hydrangeas look down upon the roses and lavender.

The prevailing impression of the garden at Arbigland is one of peace and remoteness. While it will give restful pleasure to the general lover of gardens, it has an additional feature of interest to the specialist. A few years ago, a land survey group was engaged to map and catalogue the entire garden. A copy of the resulting data is kept in the house, but from it a former lecturer in Ornamental Horticulture at Reading University compiled and checked on the ground a list of Arbigland's 'Top 100' plants, a task that took her a year. It is available at the cost of a few pence to visitors and is well worth such modest expenditure, for not only are the plants listed with their country of origin, but the dates when they were first introduced to this country are also given.

ARDANAISEIG, by Kilchrenan, Taynuilt

Owners: Mr and Mrs J Smith

Turn off A85 at Taynuilt. B845 to Kilchrenan, from where signposted

1 April to 31 October during daylight hours

The remote Scottish Baronial-style mansion of Ardanaiseig was built for Colonel James Archibald Campbell in 1834, by the Scottish architect William Burn. It was then called New Inverewe, Colonel Campbell being a nephew of the Archibald Campbell whose ancestors had owned Inverewe estate since the 14th century. Colonel Campbell had a large family, especially of daughters, whom he apparently ruled with all the strictness of a devout Victorian Christian. On his death in 1879, the estate was sold to John Ainsworth, who had interests in coal, iron and heavy industry in Cumberland, on condition that the name was changed to Ardanaiseig ('the point of the ferry'), the new owner not being a Campbell. In due course, Ainsworth became Liberal member of Parliament for Argyll and was given a Baronetcy for public services. His son, Sir Thomas, succeeded him but moved to Ireland in 1947, where he created another garden. Ardanaiseig was then sold to Sir Duncan McCallum, Conservative member of Parliament for Argyll and son of 'Charles Coborn', who won music-hall fame with *The Man who Broke the Bank at Monte Carlo*. Sir Duncan died in 1958 and in 1963 his widow sold the estate to the present owners, who in 1979–80 turned it into a luxurious hotel, offering magnificent views across Loch Awe to Ben Lui and Ben Cruachan.

While the garden does not enjoy the benefit of the Gulf Stream, the climate is mild and the soil acid. Except from the east wind that blows across Loch Awe, the gardens are well sheltered by woodland. It is, indeed, fundamentally a woodland garden. A stream running along the main drive issues from a little lily-pond beside the path that leads to the walled garden. A large sycamore tree facing the hotel is covered with polypodium (a type of fern) firmly rooted in its ancient bark. The walled garden, when we saw it, showed signs of having been well laid out and to have contained interesting plants. Alas, as so often in these days of financial restriction, it is now somewhat overgrown. Pink erinus grows everywhere on the walls. The orchard section contains plum, apple and pear trees as well as a Judas tree, *Cercis siliquastrum*, common enough in England, but a comparative rarity in Scotland.

The main glory of the garden, however, is undoubtedly its azaleas and rhododendrons—the large-leafed *R falconeri*, the *R sinogrande* species and some fine examples of *R calophytum*. Many of the splendid trees date from the time when the house was built, and have achieved enormous stature. There are several species of nothofagus, many different maples—the Canadian maples were planted to commemorate the centenary of the Confederation of Canada—cercidiphyllum, enkianthus, hoheria and, among the more recent plantings, *Taxodium distichum* and *Metasequoia glyptostroboides*. The conifers include a Sitka spruce 132 feet by 20 feet, and large specimens of *Abies nordmanniana, A grandis*, and *A procera*. Here, too, are *Pinus radiata, Pseudotsuga* and *Wellingtonia*.

There was once a formal garden in front of the house, but the former lawns have long since merged with the woodland, inclining towards the reedy shore of Loch Awe. Like so many West Highland gardens, this one achieves the peak of its glory when the floor of the woodlands is successively carpeted with snowdrops, daffodils and bluebells, and the rhododendrons and azaleas display their full effulgent colour.

ARDCHATTAN PRIORY, Loch Etive

Owner: Lieutenant-Colonel R Campbell-Preston OBE MC DL

5 miles east of the north side of Connel Bridge on the Bonawe road

1 April (or Easter, whichever is the earlier) to 31 October from 0900 hours to 2100 hours

Ardchattan Priory, the second-oldest inhabited house in Scotland, was founded in 1230 for monks of the Valliscaulian order (whose mother house was at Val des Choux — 'Kail Valley' — in Burgundy, France) by Sir Duncan MacKowle or MacDougal of the family of the then Lords of Lorn. Kail leaves, an allusion to the Order's birthplace, are carved in various places within and outwith the Priory. Only three Valliscaulian Priories existed outside France, the other two being at Beauly, now a ruin in the care of Historic Scotland, and Pluscarden, which came under Benedictine Rule in 1454, remained so until the Reformation, and has been restored and reoccupied during the 20th century. The absence of an English connection is said to have particularly endeared the Valliscaulian Order to Alexander II.

It is said that King Robert the Bruce held a Parliament at Ardchattan in 1308 and that it was the last Parliament at which Gaelic was spoken. After the Reformation, Ardchattan's last religious head (a Campbell) retained it when it became a private house in 1560. There are two versions of what happened next. The official one is that one of his descendants was against Cromwell, and that Cromwellian troops burned the Priory, leaving only the Prior's Lodging, a few fragments incorporated in the Victorian house, and the ruins of the Chapel (now cared for by Historic Scotland) containing Celtic recumbant tombs, including those marking the resting-place of MacDougal Priors and dated 1500 and 1502. The other version is that it was the Macdonalds under their leader, Colkitto, who in 1644 set fire to the Priory. In 1964, however, the historian Dr Douglas Simpson came upon a record of the burning of Ardchattan in the form of a despatch sent by Colonel Lilburne to Major-General Lambert on 14 February 1654: 'Nor was Captaine Mutloe in the Westerne Highlands idle, for hearing that the Laird Archatan (being one of the chief malignants in

Lorne) had garrison'd his house for the Enemy, he drew forth a partie out of Dunstaffenage and Dunolly, fell upon the house, and after some dispute having killed 3 of the Enemy, entered the house, and took a Lieutenant with some prisoners, and a store of armes and ammunition.'

The garden of three acres, first laid out in 1830, is separated from Loch Etive only by the narrow road beyond the wall and the shingly beach. The climate, however, is normally mild. About half of the garden is formal—that part in front of the house and along the west side—having two herbaceous borders, a rose border, a rock garden and two shrub borders.

The main herbaceous border runs at right angles to the house down towards the shore wall and contains colourful examples of the customary perennials.

On the bank beneath the terrace on which the house stands is one of the shrub borders, containing among other specimens, *Hebe traversii, H recurva* and *H* 'Pagei'. Running up the east side of the house and facing the rose garden across the upper lawn is the rock garden, rich with edelweiss and *Leucanthemum hosmariense*.

A mixed border features *Rosa* 'Cornelia', *R* 'Penelope', *R* 'Felicity' and the polyantha rose, 'Stephen Langdon', along with euphorbias and a yellow clematis clambering up the wall behind the border.

To the west of the house is a wood the ground of which is seasonally covered with daffodils. Two corners contain plots of azaleas, linked by a shrub walk. Along the bottom of the wood, between the Monks' Walk and the wall beside the wood, there are rhododendrons, philadelphus, embothrium and *Enkianthus campanulatus*.

There is another shrub garden beside the now drained and grassed Monks' Pond. Indeed, the garden contains over 200 varieties of shrubs, including viburnums, *Mahonia bealii, Crindodendron hookerianum*, the Chilean Lantern tree, *Hoheria lyallii, Cotoneaster bullatus* and the spectacular *Berberis linearifolia*, as well as some well-established rowan trees, or sorbus. Towards the back of the garden beyond the Monks' Pond, there have been recently planted 18 different varieties of sorbus, which face a row of *Pyrus salicifolia pendula*, with their beautiful silvery-green leaves. Here, too, are hydrangeas and climbing roses. There are numerous other fine trees of great age, including yews and sycamores, some, indeed, over 400 years old.

The views down Loch Etive, with the hills of Mull in the background, and up towards Ben Cruachan are spectacular, making a visit to pleasant Ardchattan scenically as well as horticulturally an experience not to be missed.

ARDTORNISH, Morvern, by Lochaline

Owner: Ardtornish Estate Company Limited

Off A884, 2 miles north-north-east of Lochaline

1 April to 31 October
from 1000 hours to 1800 hours

The house and garden of Ardtornish, with magnificent views along Loch Aline and across to the island of Mull, take their name from a ruined castle on a nearby basaltic headland on the Sound of Mull, at the east side of the entrance to Loch Aline, once a stronghold of the Lords of the Isles and which features in Sir Walter Scott's last epic poem, *The Lord of the Isles.*

The site of Ardtornish House was chosen by a London distiller, Octavius Smith, in 1856. He built himself a house which, however, was taken down by his son, Valentine Smith, to make way for the present mansion, completed in 1891 by the Inverness architect, Alexander Ross. The garden of some 28 acres was laid out by Valentine Smith, his successors, and by his sister Gertrude and her son, Gerard Craig Sellar. The garden at that time took the form of a rocky ravine with several mown lawns, rockeries and streams planted with various species of hosta, crocosmia, spiraea and lysichitum, as well as escallonia, enkianthus and embothrium. The rather ordinary rhododendrons were set out on a cliff behind the house and on a steep glen to the west of the garden. Once, 12 gardeners were employed. Apprentices became heads of the Parks Departments in, amongst other places, Glasgow and Manchester.

In 1930, Ardtornish was bought by Owen and Emmeline Hugh Smith, who planted a wider range of shrubs in a less formal style. They had greatly admired some of the species grown in Kiloran Garden on the Isle of Colonsay. It, of course, enjoys the benefits of the Gulf Stream, which Ardtornish does not; but the Smith successes did include plantings of *Eucryphia x nymansensis* 'Nymansay', on a bank to the south-west of the house, and lovely specimens of *Hoheria lyallii* up the driveway, as well as many acers and a range of sorbus species. The variety of rhododendrons was also greatly extended, particularly after Mr Smith's death in 1958, when his widow added *ambiguum, campylo-carpum, cinnabarinum, blandfordiiflorum* and *roylei, decorum, oreotrephes, souliei, yakushimanum* in variety and *R* 'Polar Bear' for late summer colour. There are also many hybrid azaleas from Pollok House, Glasgow. The garden is now in the care of Mr and Mrs Smith's daughter, Mrs Faith Raven.

The shade-preferring primula garden has been extended to include variegated hostas and *Meconopsis betonicifolia*. There are also many fine conifers and other splendid examples of mature shrubs and trees.

The interest in the garden runs through its display of early-flowering rhododendrons and daffodils in April and bluebells in May and June, to the glorious colourings of acers, berberis and cercidiphyllum in October. Like so many west coast Highland gardens, however, it is a woodland garden at its best in May and June.

ARDUAINE

Owner: The National Trust for Scotland

3 miles from Kilmelford on A816 Oban to Lochgil-phead road

Late May to early August
from 0930 hours to 1800 hours

Arduaine is Gaelic for 'green point', or 'headland'. In 1897, James Arthur Campbell and his wife bought Asknish Farm, by Asknish Bay, Loch Melfort, to make their home. The headland was then dominated by heather, rushes and bracken. In 1905, they knocked down the farm and built Arduaine House, with its splendid vistas down Loch Melfort. Two years before, they had begun to create their garden in a hollow in the lea of the headland, which to some extent broke the force of the westerly winds and where springs supplied clear water.

In 1907, the Campbells were the guests of Osgood Mackenzie at Inverewe. He had pioneered the technique of successfully planting up an exposed west coast site (where, nevertheless, the climate is otherwise relatively mild because of the Gulf Stream), by the provision of a shelter-belt to give protection from the salt-laden winds. So, in 1908, Campbell planted 2 000 Japanese larch seedlings, which now provide the principal shelter for the plant collection. By 1920, the main woodland was planted. Seeds of rare plants were brought back from China, along with cargoes of tea.

James Campbell died in 1929. Though the estate changed hands several times during the ensuing decade, James's son, Bruce, continued to develop the garden which in its 30s heyday employed no fewer than six gardeners. Work came to a standstill during World War II, after which James's grandson, Major Iain Campbell, did his best to keep the garden going with a much reduced labour force. This, however, included his children's nanny, Miss Yule. When the children who had been her charges grew up, she devoted all her energies to the garden; so enthusiastically, indeed, that sometimes after daylight had gone, someone had to be despatched to find her with the aid of a torch.

Miss Yule finally retired in 1964, the year in which the house was sold to become the Loch Melfort Hotel. The great storm of 1968 caused havoc among the trees in the shelter-belt protecting the now-neglected garden.

In 1971, two brothers from Essex, Edmund and Harry Wright, took it over, by which time they had to clear a wilderness of thorns, weeds and fallen trees. They then redesigned damaged areas, thinning trees in the woodland section to allow more light to penetrate, and extending or creating rock gardens, a water garden, a stream garden and a cliff garden, in all covering 14 acres. As a result, Arduaine became a garden in the 'grand style', which every true plantsman would covet.

After 20 years' hard labour, however, the Wright brothers in 1992 handed over the garden into the safe keeping of the National Trust for Scotland, who accepted it because of its quality and national importance. The Trust has begun the task of preservation and, where necessary, restoration with its customary care for the original design.

Rhododendrons are the principal glory of this garden. There are magnificent exhibits of *R giganteum* — one, indeed, the largest we have ever seen in Britain — *R sinogrande, R rex, R fulvum, R griffithianum, R cinnabarinum roylei* and, resembling a tree, *R arboreum*. There is also *R fictolacteum*, with which the Wrights achieved exhibition success and, grown from seed imported from Sri Lanka, *R zeylanicum*.

Magnolias also play an important role at Arduaine. Here may be seen the sweet-scented *M obovata, M sieboldii* and *M denudata*, rich in its flowering (and, incidentally, the 'Yulan' of Chinese temple gardens). Several *Eucalyptus gunnii* grow here to a great height. From New Zealand, there is the leathery-leaved *Griselinia littoralis* which also thrives, as does the thick-stemmed creeper, *Berberidopsis corallina*. The Handkerchief tree, *Davidia vilmoriniana*, planted by the Wrights, is said to be the largest in Scotland. Other notable specimens that flourish include *Berberis darwinii, Euphorbia mellifera* and *Olearia macrodonta* and the more unusual form, *O insignis*.

Following either a blue arrow path or a wider-routed green path, the visitor can choose to explore only the main garden, or take in as well 'Miss Yule's Rockery', the Round Pond and the Herons' Pond. As the National Trust's guide leaflet so succinctly puts it: 'The visitor is led through a series of compartmented garden areas of informal lawns and shrubberies, then drawn on, rising almost imperceptibly, to the wilder woodland garden on the heights beyond . . . A side-path through the shelter-belt leads to a viewpoint overlooking the contrasting wild countryside . . . A disguised internal viewpoint suddenly opens up a bird's-eye view over the lower garden, showing at a glance its brilliant tapestry of colours and textures.' These include in spring golden carpets of miniature daffodils, *Narcissus cyclamineus*.

Rosa 'MEG'

ARDWELL HOUSE, Ardwell

Owners: Frank and Francis Brewis

10 miles south of Stranraer on A716 to Drummore

1 March to 31 October
from 1000 hours to 1800 hours

Ardwell House was built between 1720 and 1740, added to in Victorian times and remodelled back to its original Georgian proportions in 1956. There was an older fortified dwelling once on the site, its defensive moat lying to the east of the present house.

There is an island feeling about the Rhins of Galloway, that peninsula which reaches into the Irish Sea north and south from the mainland at Stranraer, combining softer contours than the Highlands, a lusher growth, yet something of the same close association with the open reflections of sea and sky. Nowhere is this peculiar quality more attractive than at Ardwell.

The garden covers five acres, situated between Luce Bay and the Irish Sea. Much of it is natural in character, though there is a 'front' garden, to the side of the house, and a walled garden 200 or so yards away. When the present owners took over the estate in 1949, the garden had suffered neglect for some years and there was much clearing of weeds and scrub to be accomplished. Many sapling trees were also planted at that time. The replanning of the garden was then designed to provide a continuity of colour throughout the year, from the arrival of the snowdrops, winter aconites and the winter-flowering *Erica carnea* to the brilliant show of April daffodils. Later, azaleas, flowering cherries and rhododendrons follow in early May.

In June, the rockplants are in flower — blue campanulas, dianthus in various shades, saxifrage, stonecrop, thymes, aubretias and other low-growing colourful plants creep along finding congenial homes in the nooks and crannies.

The herbaceous border has a variety of roses in early summer with, in August, hydrangeas, a wide selection of other perennials and late-flowering heathers. Later still, these are followed by colchicums and Autumn crocuses. The park is well-planted with mature trees having colourful autumn foliage.

In the walled garden, cattle graze placidly in their fenced-off areas, but the rest of it, partly compartmented with little walls, is cultivated. Many of the plants are propagated here and are for sale.

The garden includes two ponds. A walk round the larger one rewards the visitor with fine views over Luce Bay to Port William and Whithorn and westwards to the Irish Sea.

BALMORAL CASTLE, Deeside

Owner: Her Majesty the Queen

Crathie

May, June and July from 1000 hours to 1700 hours

The personal Scottish Highland home of Her Majesty the Queen stands on a strip of level meadow on one side of a sweeping curve of the River Dee. Balmoral (in Gaelic, 'majestic dwelling') stands on the site of a smaller castle owned by Sir Robert Gordon, who was related to Sir James Clark, physician to Queen Victoria. When Sir Robert died, the lease (held by the Earl of Fife) was secured for the Queen and Prince Albert in February 1848. In September, they took possession of their 'pretty little castle in the old Scottish style', parts of which were over 200 years old. By 1852, the royal family had purchased the land on which Balmoral stood, along with the neighbouring estates of Birkhall and Abergeldie.

Soon, however, the castle proved too small for their growing family. William Smith of Aberdeen built for them the present castle 100 yards to the north-west of the old castle, which they continued to occupy until the new castle was ready when they arrived at Balmoral in the autumn of 1855.

Queen Victoria called Balmoral 'this dear paradise', and she and Albert lost no time in creating a garden about the castle, planting the grounds with rare conifers and forest trees. The half-mile drive into the castle, for instance, has trees probably planted by Albert, including *Abies grandis, Abies concolor var lowiana, Abies alba* and *Tsuga heterophylla,* amongst others. There is also a *Picea glauca var* 'Albertiana' planted by Queen Mary after World War I on the left side of the road. She also added the sunken Rose Garden in 1932 and since 1953 the Queen and Prince Philip have made further extensions, including the Water Garden near Victoria's Garden Cottage.

In all, the gardens cover three acres. The broad herbaceous borders and the rose garden are so designed as to provide the maximum colour from mid-August to October, when the Royal Family is in residence.

In the grounds there is a very handsome flower garden conservatory, as well as numerous statues, monuments and cairns to Queen Victoria's family and their descendants. Victoria and Albert are themselves commemorated by two statues gifted in 1887 by the Balmoral tenantry. Particularly charming is the chamois statue and fountain.

From the rear entrance there is a beautiful riverside walk, leading to the stables (now mostly garages, although three still house ponies), the kennels and the game larders. Included in the policies is Loch Muick, where Queen Victoria loved to picnic, although she observed the name means '*pig, not* a pretty name'. The area around the loch is now run as a nature reserve in conjunction with the Scottish Wildlife Trust. It is freely open to the public, except during the stalking season, when warning notices are placed at all access points.

BARGANY, Ayrshire

Owner: Captain North Dalrymple Hamilton

3 miles east of Girvan, on B734, off A77 Girvan to Ayr road

1 March to 31 October daily
from 1000 hours to 1900 hours

This was once Kennedy of Bargany land. The Kennedys of Bargany lived in a castle, on the River Girvan, not a trace of which remains, and apparently spent much of their time feuding with their kinsfolk, the Kennedys of Cassillis. The present Bargany mansion was built about 1681, the initials of its first owner, H B (Hamilton of Bargany), still to be seen above the front door.

Many famous landscape architects were involved in the making of the gardens during the 18th and 19th centuries: the great architect William Adam, William Boutcher, Thomas White the younger, George Robertson and George Hay, who designed the walled garden, now, alas, a nettle-thick grassy wilderness. Outside two of its walls, however, there are smallish gardens and down a third is a path lined with large shrubs such as philadelphus, viburnum, magnolia, pieris and mahonia.

In the section nearest the Keeper's house, there are several magnificent specimens of the Chilean Fire tree, *Embothrium coccineum,* and azaleas. Four delightful little stone figures playing, respectively, a flute, tambourine, mandolin and aeolian harp face its semi-circular shape.

Outside the long wall at the opposite extremity, there is a large bed of Kurume azaleas with, at right angles to it, a grassy path lined on both sides with cherry trees.

Snowdrops, followed by daffodils, make spectacular displays in the woodland garden, at its finest from March to early May, when the many varieties of rhododendrons and azaleas, which line the long avenues, are in magnificent bloom.

About 1910, Colonel Sir North Dalrymple Hamilton had the woodland garden, through which a rocky stream tumbles, laid out. The most striking feature is

still the lily-pond, really a small lake, which is surrounded by large Ponticum azaleas, *Rhododendron
luteum,* and clumps of *Azalea mollis* 'Ghent', together
with hybrid rhododendrons.

The garden is also spectacular when autumn colours
the trees, many of which are a very considerable age.
Beeches and conifers abound, and rare species include
the Handkerchief tree, *Davidia involucrata,* the Maidenhair tree, *Gingko biloba,* and the Fossil tree, *Metasequoia glyptostroboides.* The extensive gardens and the
park are, indeed, a paradise for tree-lovers, though
once its spring and early summer glories have faded,
other garden-lovers may, perhaps, wish they could have
seen it in its high Edwardian heyday.

Davidia involucrata

BARGUILLEAN, Taynuilt

Owners: Mr and Mrs Neil MacDonald

3 miles north-west of Taynuilt, on the Glen Lonan road

1 April to 31 October
from 1800 hours to 2100 hours

The nine acres of the natural garden at Barguillean Farm were conceived by Neil and Betty MacDonald as a memorial to their son, Angus, shot dead in the streets of Cyprus in 1956, during the years of unrest, for no obvious reason, while he was acting as a reporter. The approach to Barguillean, up Glen Lonan, yields up some superb mountain views at every turn of the narrow road.

The garden covers the quite steeply sloping southern bank of a pre-existing artificial loch, on the surface of which now float great patches of water-lilies. By chance, the loch had already been named Loch Angus, after Angus MacCallum, the ghillie who, in 1906, suggested damming a burn to improve the trout fishing.

Beyond the loch and the pond—a feature that took Neil MacDonald 13 years to dig, leaving an island in the middle planted with the Exbury azalea—there is nothing formal about Barguillean, not even the marked paths, thus leaving the visitor free to wander where he or she will. There are over 200 hybrid azaleas flourishing where the slopes afford sufficient protection, and, amidst the birches, oaks and conifers on the hillside, more than 250 rhododendrons. These include *Rhododendron neriiflorum, R lodor, R insigne, R rex* and *R rubiginosum*, some examples, like the azaleas, flourishing over a period of about eight months.

The MacDonalds' younger son, Sam, in 1977 set up Barguillean Nurseries Limited near the garden. He stocks more than 300 varieties of trees and shrubs, supplying landowners and garden centres.

BELL'S CHERRYBANK GARDENS, Perth

Owner: United Distillers UK

Off A9 Glasgow to Perth road and right at Cherrybank

Daily until mid-October

There cannot be many companies whose offices are surrounded by 18 acres of splendidly laid-out and immaculately kept gardens, which slope to a busy trunk road, in this case leading into the City of Perth. Indeed, the main Water Garden runs parallel to the road and is separated from it only by a bank and a very attractive wrought-iron fence. The visitor could be forgiven for imagining the noise of heavy traffic so close by would remove any pleasure the garden could afford. Not so. This is a garden of colour and tranquillity where ducks, dippers, herons and kingfishers (alas, we did not see the last two) dabble or flit in among the bullrushes.

In 1973, the offices of Arthur Bell and Son were moved to the present Cherrybank location which had been simply and naturally laid out. The original concept was to have 11 acres transformed into a fine garden. To this end, Robert Matthew/Johnson-Marshall-Sportwork were given the huge task of planting 45 000 shrubs and 1 200 trees which have now matured into a splendid garden, the recipient in 1982 of a Civic Trust Award. It has subsequently received other distinguished awards.

A seven-acre extension—the Bell's Cherrybank Gardens—was added in 1984 and again designed by Robert Matthew/Johnson-Marshall, the work being carried out this time by J D Minto. This part of the estate is very largely devoted to the growing of heathers and has won for itself the accolade of the National Heather Collection. It is maintained in co-operation with the National Council for the Conservation of Plants and Gardens, under the guidance of the Northern Horticultural Society, based at Harlow Carr Botanical Gardens in Harrogate. Hazel Huddlestone designed the remarkable collection (which today embraces over 800 varieties of heather and includes as many cultivars as possible of Bruckenthalia, Calluna, Daboecia and the hardy European species of Erica), gathered from all over the world. The collection is being constantly added to, the ultimate aim being to possess at least 1000 varieties.

The two gardens merge into each other, thus providing a harmonious whole, each one being linked by grassy slopes, hedges and appropriate shrubs or trees. Water is a feature of both areas.

The approach to the Bell's Heather Garden is through the little tea-room from the windows of which there is a magnificent view of the slopes and beds containing every colour of leaf and flower. Indeed, the whole resembles a spectacular oriental carpet. The beds are of irregular shape and size but each contains 30 to 40 specimens of several varieties. This is a garden which has colour throughout the year, if not from the flowers (many of which are winter-flowering) then from the foliage in every shade of green, silver, gold, or even apricot.

The eye is delighted as well. There is a doocot where fantails proudly strut; a trellis garden featuring a set of tubular bells on which the visitor is invited to play; a miniature Crystal Palace containing budgerigars and cockatiels sufficiently at home to be nesting in the upper reaches; a variety of sculptures by Laurence Broderick and one by Iain McIntosh of a girl washing her hair in the Acoustic Pool. If one stands immediately in front of the spouting water, its tone changes to a sonorous note. The children are not forgotten and have their own play area.

A break in the hedge gives access to the larger section of the garden, the original area. Beside the offices there is a 22½-tonne mosaic by Sadie McLellan which contains the motto *Nunc et Semper* (Now and Always). The same artist has also devised a fascinating sculpture depicting the Sun, Moon, Earth and Seed. The whole moves round silently and majestically and as it turns, falling rain and growing seed can be identified in the stained glass. Nearby there is a group of silver birches of the *jacquemontii* variety, and a bed of low-growing *Pinus mugo*.

As visitors proceed down the immaculate grassy slope, they will see Ian Hamilton Finlay's sundial in the form of an eye. The nearby wishing well is a perhaps less happy addition to the garden, but serves its purpose in that all coins thrown down it are donated to charity, as are the contents of the collection boxes. Continuing downward, one comes to a lily-pond surrounded by clumps of bergenia and astilbe. The natural valley here contains colourful herbaceous borders and along the riverside, spirea and potentilla flourish. A little island is planted with vigorous *Alchemilla mollis*. The predominating yellows come also from mimulus, irises and Himalayan cowslips.

The gardens also contain, appropriately, a large bed of the whisky-coloured 'Johnnie Walker' rose and a heath-planting in the shape of a bell.

Nymphaea x marliacea

BLAIRHOYLE, Thornhill

Owner: Ian Stirling, the garden created by the late Lieutenant-Colonel I D and the late Mrs Patullo

A873 Stirling to Aberfoyle road, 3½ miles west of Thornhill

At present by arrangement only

The 17-acre garden of Blairhoyle was first laid out about a century ago by Mr George Crabbie, of Crabbie's Ginger Wine fame, with advice from an expert from the Botanic Gardens in Edinburgh. When the late Lieutenant-Colonel and Mrs Patullo bought Blairhoyle in 1968, they found both the garden and the walled garden overgrown; indeed, semi-derelict. With only a little part-time labour they set about restoring it, and now, largely due to the heroic efforts of the deceased couple, it is one of the most immaculate gardens in the west of Scotland; a garden for everyone, because of the variety and rarity of its plant life, and a riot of both vivid and subtle colour throughout the year.

From the long wall at the back of the house, the near view takes in the slope of the garden down to the lake — created by the Crabbies but subsequently silted up and restored by the Patullos — round which the path winds, at the end of which by the lakeside are two lovely Weeping limes. In the middle distance, there is a splendid prospect of Flanders Moss with, beyond the Fintry Hills, the Campsie Fells.

A long avenue of splendid lime trees bisects an arboretum planted about 100 years ago which contains many rare trees. Here you will find the Yellow birch, *Betula lutea*; the Wing-Nut tree, *Pterocarya caucasica*; the Eagle-Claw Maple, *Acer platanoides laciniatum*; the Katsura tree, *Cercidiphyllum japonicum*; the Sweet Gum, *Liquidambar styraciflua*; the Japanese Red cedar, *Cryptomeria japonica*; the Cut-Leaf beech, *Fagus sylvatica heterophylla* and also a marvellous Tri-coloured beech. So impressive, indeed, is the variety of trees in the garden that the International Society of Dendrologists visited Blairhoyle in 1967. To the left of the arboretum beside a lawn, there is a plot ablaze with Candelabra primulas, prunella and other plants.

Then there are the succeeding spectacular displays: snowdrops in the woodland; carpets of many-coloured crocuses; Winter heaths and, early in April, 'a host of golden daffodils' enriching the grassy stretch in front of the house. In May, bluebells, *Endymion non-scriptus*, take over, to be followed by a wealth of azaleas, rhododendrons and early roses.

Following the driveway lower down the slope to the right of the house, there is a curving path leading to a corner which in June is a mass of many-hued Candelabra primulas, alpines, hostas and other delights, as well as a strategically placed seat from which to drink in this glory of colour and shape.

To the left of the house is the walled garden, outside of which a burn (which can be crossed by a charming arched wooden bridge) tumbles down through ferns and other greenery to the lower slopes, where Mrs Patullo planted on both sides magnificent stretches of heaths of every kind.

The walled garden also slopes down and is roughly divided into three sections. In the section where the greenhouses are located — and in which, incidentally, Mrs Patullo propagated a huge number of cuttings for charity and her own use — are two colourful herbaceous borders. A rose-covered arbour entwined with honeysuckles is a feature of the lower lawn, which runs the breadth of the walled garden. Here, again, there is a further source of delight. A broad alpine border has been built up at the back of the lawn and contains all kinds of lovely plants including various charming miniature penstemons. A welcome feature of this garden is that plants, especially the most important ones, because of efficient labelling, can be easily identified.

BRANKLYN

Owner: The National Trust for Scotland

¼ mile from the Queen's Bridge, Perth, on A75 Perth–Dundee road

Daily between 1 March and 31 October from 1000 hours to sunset

Branklyn is a 20th-century garden of about two acres, laid out on a west-facing slope overlooking the River Tay. It is the creation of two enthusiasts, Dorothy and John Renton, who in 1922 bought a small, fairly steep piece of ground from Orchardton Nursery, and built a house on it. They then proceeded to lay out a garden.

Mrs Renton was a modest expert who in 1954 was awarded the Veitch Memorial Medal (inaugurated in 1870) from the Royal Horticultural Society for her achievement at Branklyn, and in 1960 the Scottish Horticultural Society Medal from the Royal Caledonian Horticultural Society. Her husband was a chartered land surveyor who became, amongst other things, Chairman of the Agricultural Executive for Eastern Scotland and in 1952 a CBE. She, he maintained, was the real gardener; he, partly designer, but mostly, in his own phrase, 'the willing labourer'.

According to Dorothy Renton, who was perhaps influenced by the 'complementary plant association' ideas of Gertrude Jekyll, there was no overall design for the garden. It was simply to be 'a home from home for plants', many of them rare and exciting varieties.

The upper and lower paths of this garden, beautiful at any time of the year, form its framework and are linked by further narrow winding paths among the irregularly shaped plots and grassy approaches.

The lower path runs beside the beech hedge, built to shut off the garden from the traffic on the Perth–Dundee road, much busier and noisier than it would have been in the time of the Rentons. This path winds past their earliest rock-work, the first scree garden, the cascade and the pool.

The second and largest rock garden, finished in 1925,

lies near the house, a little to the south, and is in many ways the centrepiece of the whole ensemble. Stones had to be brought from nearby Kinnoul Hill by steam-engine, and a team of men with crowbars levered them into place. It has recently been rebuilt, with loving attention given to replacing the specimens to which Dorothy Renton was devoted. Her own collection of rock and bulbous plants was known internationally for its rarity and difficulty of cultivation, but which she managed with ease and to the envy of her many admirers. Some of her original plants have been propagated and are now back in their place of origin.

Still further south, the third rock garden is of limestone scree and accommodates those plants which require alkaline conditions. Here Mrs Renton established to perfection the rare *Paraquilegia anemonoides*, or Blue buttercup, as well as primulas, gentians and saxifrages, also to be found elsewhere in the garden.

A feature at the south end of the garden, twice extended by the Rentons, are several peat-wall beds. Peat-wall gardening originated in the 1920s at Logan House, although there, turf was used. A decade or so later, the problem of seeding grass was overcome at the Royal Botanic Garden in Edinburgh by using blocks of peat instead of turf, an example that was quickly followed by the Rentons at Branklyn. In this section numerous varieties of rhododendrons and other Sino-Himalayan plants flourish, as well as cassiopes (of which Branklyn holds the National Collection). A magnificent spread of meconopsis, ranging from the stately *Meconopsis sheldonii* of glowing blue, to the less tall forms such as *grandis,* and the lovely white *betonicifolia alba* predominate. Candelabra primulas have seeded themselves in amongst such plants as trillium (including the lovely form, *cuneatum*) and phyllodoce.

From the upper path, delightful groupings and colourful vistas abound, each accessible for detailed plant examination. Here in the irregularly shaped plots, may be found a profusion of flowers, including the Branklyn paeony and a group of acers which provide glowing autumnal colour as does the *Cercidiphyllum japonicum*, which also pervades the air with its straw-berry-like perfume. At the same time, colchicums and gentians provide additional colour.

In early summer, several *Viburnum plicatum* 'Mariesii' spread their white umbrellas over many choice specimens beneath. Other plants of interest are to be found in troughs. These include *Gentiana gelida*, *Helychrysom milfordiae* and *Pygmaea pulvinaris*.

The distant view across the Tay valley has changed with the years. When the Rentons first began to lay out their garden, they must have looked over to a green hill. In post-war years it has been covered with closely-packed suburban housing. The atmosphere of the garden nevertheless contains its own tranquillity, in May drenched in a variety of delightful scents.

Dorothy Renton died in 1966 and her husband the following year. Many of the rare plants they had so lovingly collected over more than 40 years disappeared as a result of the enforced neglect brought about by their final illnesses. John bequeathed Branklyn to the National Trust for Scotland, who accepted it in 1968. As is their wont, the Trust has replaced much that was lost, and taken great care to ensure that, as far as possible, the garden, and its more than 3000 or so plants to delight the visitor, remains true to the Rentons' conception of it.

BRECHIN CASTLE

Owners: The Earl and Countess of Dalhousie

Brechin 1 mile on A94 road

*One Sunday in May and one Sunday in June. For dates **The Gardens of Scotland** handbook should be consulted*

The old fortress, which stood on the site of what is now Brechin Castle, was besieged by the forces of Edward I in 1303 and only surrendered when its commander, Sir Thomas Maule, was killed by a missile. That old fortress, on a rock above the South Esk river, was replaced by the castle of 1711, built by Alexander Edward. Alterations and additions were made by John Henderson of Edinburgh in 1854 and again in 1863.

In 1715, James VIII was proclaimed by James, 4th Earl of Panmure and Baron Maule of Brechin and Navar. On the collapse of the 1715 Jacobite rising, the estates were forfeited, being bought back in 1764 by William Maule, Earl of Panmure and Forth, on whose death in 1782 they passed to his nephew, George Ramsay, 8th Earl of Dalhousie and ancestor of the present owner.

The walled garden of about 13 acres was created by the first Baron Panmure shortly after 1800, and is heart-shaped. The walls enclosing it were built by Lady Panmure during the 18th century. At least 10 of the trees she planted have survived: two *Cedrus libani* and eight *Fagus sylvatica purpurea*. Rather surprisingly, the banker Sir William Forbes, a friend of the then owner, thought that 'the whole being laid out in sweeps and curves . . . produces the most monotonous effect.' That is not a view that would be endorsed today, whether on account of the roses on the walls on either side of the elaborate garden gate—they include *Rosa foetida* 'bicolour', otherwise known as 'Austrian Copper' and the vivid buttercup-yellow, single flowers of *Rosa ecae*, named after the initials of the wife of the Dr Aitchison who introduced the shrub from Afghanistan in 1880—or in the face of the wonderful display of Tree paeonies, their white, purple and pink flowers lighting the early summer days. Other fine plants include a *Cytisus battandieri*, from Morocco, a member of the broom family, and against the wall, a splendid *Clematis*

'Etoile Rose'. Four impressive examples of Lawson's cypress flank the wide gravel path that forms the main axis of the walled garden. To the left, through a gap in the castellated yew hedge, a flight of steps flanked by cherubs leads to a circular pool. To the right, a path leads to an alcove in which there is a drinking fountain carrying the inscription: 'Drink and be Thankful'. A door leads to the nursery greenhouses, put up in one of the bays in the heart shape about 1820, and now housing peaches, figs and grapevines, as well as *Lapageria rosea* (the Chilean Bell-flower), *Passiflora caerulea* (Passion flower), *Rhododendron dalhousiae*, named after the wife of the 10th Earl of Dalhousie, who was the last Governor-General of India, some cymbidium hybrids and also sweetly-scented azaleas.

Shelter is provided for the garden by ancient holly and yew hedges—one of the latter with a tunnel through the centre—and by mature beech, oak, Douglas fir, cedars and *Sequoiadendron giganteum*.

Returning to the main path through the walled garden, the visitor comes on an unusual sculpted moondial. From where the yew hedge crosses the path, there are two low pillars carrying stone globes and a wide expanse of lawn in the other bay of the heart-shape. It contains a two-storey summer house once used for entertaining guests. Flanking seats are over-hung with clematis and honeysuckle. Nearby is a tassle bush, *Garrya elliptica*, and the hanging red flowers of a *Ribes speciosum*, espaliered against the wall. Plots contain shrub roses and lavender, as well as a collection of rhododendrons, including the hardy *R calophytum*, grown by the present owner from seed in 1952.

Coming back to the central path, a birch grove to the left is complemented by a truly magnificent effusion of massed laburnums to the right. Further along the path a stone sundial is surrounded by a box hedge and six Lawson's cypresses. Another grove to the right is of *Prunus* 'Shimidsu Sakura'. A stone urn marks the end of the upper garden.

The lower side of the garden contains a variety of splendid trees—some 300 year-old beeches, a Balkan spruce and a group of maples. A glade beyond has Himalayan poppies, including *Meconopsis grandis* 'Prain's Variety'. The lower garden is bounded by a ha-ha, now almost covered with a variety of rhododendrons, including *R loderi*.

This wooded garden leads to a formal water garden with an ornamental lily-pond. A clipped leylandii hedge forms the bottom backdrop. On the other three sides, small hedges mark off beds of tulips. A path and steps lead back to the upper garden.

While many yew hedges and *Acer palmatum atropurpureum* in the garden were planted by the owner's mother between 1920 and 1940, the present Earl and his wife decided to keep the layout but to modernise it. They therefore planted trees and shrubs with the aim of ensuring that the garden would be at its best at the end of May and throughout June — 'rhododendron and rose time consecutively', as the Earl puts it. Since the garden lies half a mile from the Castle, another of their ambitions was to 'join them up'; as a result of which there are now 'lots of azaleas (mollis) and rhododendrons, a collection of birch trees, daffodils and a new area of autumn colour'.

This is undoubtedly one of the two or three most varied and important gardens in Scotland.

Passiflora caerulea

BRODICK CASTLE GARDENS, Isle of Arran

Owner: The National Trust for Scotland

2 miles north of Brodick

Daily from 1000 hours to 1700 hours

The oldest part of Brodick Castle dates from the 13th century, when it was one of three strongholds for the defence of Arran. The English held it during the Scottish War of Independence. In the late 16th century it was a typical, if superior, example of a Scots tower-house — incidentally, Scotland's unique contribution to European architecture — to which Cromwell's troops added a battery to the east and a two-bay extension to the west. Thus it remained until 1844. The 10th Duke of Hamilton married Susan Beckford, daughter of the enormously rich art collector William Beckford of Fonthill Abbey. (The castle contains the finest Beckford collection in the country.) The 10th Duke's son, the Marquis of Douglas and Clydesdale (later the 11th Duke), married Napoleon III's cousin, Princess Marie of Baden, and commissioned James Gillespie Graham to extend the castle.

On the death of the 12th Duke in 1895, the castle passed to his only daughter, Marie Louise Hamilton (the title going to a descendant of the 4th Duke). She married the 6th Duke of Montrose in 1906. The Duke predeceased her. When she herself died in 1957, the castle and its policies were accepted by the Treasury in lieu of death duties and subsequently conveyed to the National Trust for Scotland.

There was a garden at Brodick in 1710, when what is now the wall round the modern flower garden was built. At the time of Gillespie Graham's reconstruction, a walled garden was made near the sea, but is no longer in use as such. The present garden was begun in the 1920s by the Duchess of Montrose, working together with her son-in-law, Major J P T Boscawen.

The pond and the woodland garden, covering some 60 acres, came first, a gift of rhododendrons from Muncaster Castle in Cumberland, many of them the large-leaved varieties, becoming the basis of the present collection, which now exceeds 200. There is also a group of rhododendrons gifted by Sir James Horlick from his garden in Gigha. The lower walk, which runs parallel to the main road by the sea, is lined with a screen of *R ponticum, R griffithianum* and *R montrosea-num,* named after the Duchess. In the woodland area there are many others brought in from oriental countries by such collectors as Farrer, Forrest, Kingdon-Ward and Rock. Here, too, is a collection of pink-flowering magnolia trees planted more than a quarter of a century ago.

Of the other three sections of the garden, the area round the castle has well-kept lawns and a fine range of shrubs, including a lovely *Eucryphia* 'Nymansay', *Acer campbellii, Olearia chessmanii* and *Olearia ilicifolia,* as well as a colourful selection of azalea hybrids, together with *Rhododendron occidentale,* one of the parents of the azalea family.

A door in the 1710 wall leads to the oldest part of the garden—possibly originally the vegetable garden—restored in 1982 to what it must have looked like in the 1930s. The shrubs include *Cordyline banksii, Acacia cultriformis* and a fine *Ceanothus arboreus.* The four long borders contain spring and summer bedding plants for seasonal colour, while the path at right angles, leading to a rustic arch, contains a variety of roses.

A door at the bottom of this part of the garden leads to the beautiful Pond Garden, where may be seen the huge *Gunnera manicata* at one end of the scale, so to speak, and dwarf primulas at the other. Eucryphias and the scented lily-of-the-valley tree, *Clethra arborea,* are among this area's August pleasures.

Facing the sea is the Bavarian summerhouse of 1860, with its unique ceiling adorned with patterned arrangements of various pine cones and larch rods, some stained green. A hundred years after its construction, it was restored by a party of Arran schoolchildren.

In 1958, the Duke of Montrose's daughter, Lady Jean Fforde, gifted to the National Trust a magnificent stretch of mountains and glens, including the island's highest

Culzean Castle   *Walled Garden*   *page 77*

Crathes Castle   *Rose Garden*   *page 73*

Priorwood *delphiniums* *page 167*

Branklyn *page 47*
Acer shirasawanum 'Aureum' *(back, left)*
and *Picea glauca* 'Conica' *(centre, left).*

mountain, Goatfell, and part of Glen Rosa; some 7 300 acres in all. In 1980, the policies of Brodick Castle became Scotland's first island Country Park, financially supported by both the local authority and the former Countryside Commission. These two developments greatly increase the interest for the visitor. In 1981 a full-time Ranger was employed and a Ranger Centre established in a converted poultry-house near the castle. The park, through which there are several trails, is, in the Trust's words: 'mixed woodland, part of which has been planted as a rhododendron and azalea garden'. Cuckoo pint, dog's mercury, tree lungwort lichen, wild garlic, Tunbridge filmy fern and many fungi and bluebells are to be found, as well as the Red squirrel, introduced early in the 20th century by the Duchess of Montrose. American mink, which escaped from a farm on the island just after World War II, are also sometimes to be seen. The golden eagle and the peregrine falcon are among the varied bird-life. Also attracted are buzzards and sparrowhawks by day and barn owls in the evening. During July and August that rarity in Scotland the nightjar, which lives on insects caught at night, can sometimes be seen and heard. The park incorporates the castle's old ice-house, once filled with ice collected from the mountains and lochs, or imported from Canada.

BROUGHTON HOUSE, Kirkcudbright

Owner: The National Trust for Scotland

High Street, Kirkcudbright

Daily during daylight hours

As an example of a small historic town-house garden, we have chosen that of Broughton House, Kirkcudbright. The house, which stands in the High Street of this picturesque Galloway town, was built for the Murrays of Broughton early in the 18th century and, like many large houses of its kind and time, has a 'lang rig' (long strip) garden stretching from the back of the house to the banks of the River Dee. The house's proportions are grand; it was originally used as a dower house for the laird's widow.

It was bought at the turn of the century by the bachelor artist E A Hornel, one of the 'Glasgow Boys', who did most of his work in a studio which opened on to the garden. (He specialized in rosy-cheeked children, frequently grouped in a garden setting.) He had travelled widely in Ceylon, Burma and Japan, so he landscaped Broughton House garden to make it resemble a Japanese sanctuary.

None of the plants that survive today are specifically Japanese, except perhaps the camellias. There are, however, Chinese magnolias, Himalayan honeysuckle or *Leycesteria formosa; Eucryphia glutinosa,* from Chile; Tree paeonies, *Paeonia suffruticosa,* from China and from the United States of America the Bush Anemone, *Carpentaria californica.* There are also some dwarf Japanese Stone pines, *Pinus pinea,* in stone troughs, an unusual sundial and a lead statue of a crane balanced on one leg in the water-lily pool.

The Japanese section takes up about one-third of the total garden, the other two-thirds being given over to a Scots garden, though containing such plants as early hellebores, primulas, *Daphne mezereum,* Winter jasmine, some lilacs and spiraeas including *Aruncus sylvester,* known as Goat's Beard, *Anemone elegans,* and a variety of roses including 'Albertine' which climbs up one of the walls. Other climbers include *Clematis jackmanii* and the powerfully scented *Buddleia alternifolia* from China.

Hornel bequeathed his home and its contents, including his library and pictures, along with the garden, to the people of Kirkcudbright. For many years it was cared for by the artist's Trustees and their descendants, and kept open to the public. In 1993, however, it was acquired by the National Trust for Scotland, who intend to restore the garden to its original splendour.

Camellia japonica

BUGHT FLORAL HALL, Inverness

Owner: Inverness District Council

Off Bught Road

1 April to 30 September, Monday to Friday
from 1000 hours to 2000 hours
Saturday and Sunday from 1000 hours to 1700 hours
1 October to 31 March, Monday to Sunday
from 1000 hours to dusk

On the Bught estate, the former walled garden of a now demolished mansion has been turned into a nursery for Inverness District Department of Leisure and Recreation. In large modern glasshouses, the District Council's nursery produces 130 000 summer bedding plants and 60 000 spring bedding plants, many of which may be seen here in serried ranks of brilliant colour.

Of greater interest to garden-lovers, however, will be the centrepiece, the Bught Floral Hall where, in a climatically-controlled environment, the visitor can stroll among winding paths through a sub-tropical landscape. There is a waterfall, a fountain, a tropical fish-tank and a grotto. There is also a moist section housing a good collection of ferns and a dry one featuring cacti. The Floral Hall includes many rare tropical plants, all clearly labelled. The aim is to develop a collection of disease-free, botanically healthy specimens, thus establishing an environmental resource centre.

The District Council stresses that the Floral Hall is part of a working nursery, and that professional staff are always on hand to answer queries, whether about plants in the Floral Hall, or on any other horticultural matter.

CAMBO HOUSE

Owners: Mr and Mrs Erskine
On A917 St Andrews to Crail road at Kingsbarns
Daily from 1000 hours to 1600 hours

There have been Erskines at Cambo since about 1675. The two estates of Erskine and Cambo came together under Thomas Erskine, 9th Earl of Kellie, in the late 18th century. He ran an import/export business with Sweden and was responsible for many of the Georgian steadings and farmhouses on the estate. The old house of Cambo was burnt to the ground in July 1876, following what must have been a merry staff party, while the family were away. The house was rebuilt by Wardrop and Reid between 1879 and 1881 for Sir Thomas Erskine of Cambo, and still wears a vaguely neo-Georgian aspect. An extension of 1884 includes the clock tower.

The estate of some 1600 acres sweeps down to the seashore and the Cambo Sands. It contains play areas, picnic areas, nature trails, a pets' paddock and a wide range of Scottish farm animals.

The ground floor of the house is lived in by the Erskine family. Much of the rest of the house (it contains 56 bedrooms) is occupied by students in winter and visitors in the summer, for whom there are also self-catering apartments and cottages.

The Walled Garden is approached by a long avenue of mature broadwood trees, which in some places have formed an arch over the road. At the end, it abuts on to a wide sweep of parkland where cattle graze peacefully. Outside the Walled Garden is a wild area containing teazles, some acers of recent planting, poppies and geraniums (not pelargoniums) amongst other specimens. This section leads down to a pond and into the woodland walks. A rock garden immediately outwith the Walled Garden has been planted with an interesting collection of ferns including *Polypodium vulgare*, *Asplenium trichomanes* (Maidenhair spleenwort) and *Phylitis scolopendrium* 'Crispum', which can be increased only by vegetative means.

The large Walled Garden of two acres is divided in half by a burn over which a series of delightful arched bridges takes the visitor from one side to the other. Here, there are fruit trees (plums and apples cover some of the walls), vegetables, including a handsome plot of asparagus and a nursery for young conifers, interspersed with eucalyptus saplings. In spring, the top walkway is lined by various forms of lilac. An acanthus is an attractive addition to the other perennials in the herbaceous borders on either side of one of the paths.

Vivid colour is supplied by large beds of annuals, such as nemesia, godetia and a particularly lovely deep-blue form of nigella. The colour is continued in autumn with large plantings of chrysanthemums and dahlias. A long line of paeonies supplies spring colour. Contained within one of the box-edged plots are herbs. There is a hedge of golden potentilla, a sundial and 'New Dawn' and 'Albertine' roses clamber over rustic fencing.

Considering the size of the Walled Garden and the sad state of so many such once-glorious enclosures, Cambo's is in remarkably good heart. Indeed, its tranquillity and colour were providing two lady artists with inspiration when we were there.

Geranium endressii

CARNELL, near Hurlford

Owners: Commander and Mrs J R Findlay

6 miles from Kilmarnock, 4 miles from Mauchline on A719; 1½ miles on Ayr side of A76

One day in April for the daffodils. Garden societies are welcome, if a prior arrangement has been made

The garden of Carnell, in the vicinity of Hurlford, surrounds a small, rectangular early 16th-century tower and a house by William Burn put up in 1843 for the then owner, Colonel John Ferrier Hamilton. Burn built an L-plan neo-Jacobean house with two storeys and an attic to the south-east and east of the original tower, first owned by the Wallaces of Cairn Hill (from which Carnell derives), the most famous of whom was Sir William Wallace, 'the Guardian of Scotland'. John Knox preached a sermon in the tower house, the family's piety being otherwise illustrated by the motto on a marriage lintel built into the tower wall: 'Without the Lord as Maister, he bigges (builds) in vain, be he ever so strong'.

Lilleas, the last Wallace, married her kinsman Sir Walter Sandilands Hamilton of Westport, later aide-de-camp to the Duke of Marlborough, whose most famous victory over the French was at the Battle of Blenheim in 1706, the last battle at which a British king, George II, was allowed on to the field. Commemorating the family's military involvement is a collection in the park of fragrant lime trees, laid out in the shape of the squares of Scottish infantry with their officers beside them, as the Battle of Dettingen began in 1743 (a victory commemorated, incidentally, in Handel's *Dettingen Te Deum*). The trees survive, surrounded in early spring by sheets of daffodils. Snowdrops precede them on the banks of the River Cessnock, which runs beneath the walls.

The walled garden was built in the same year as the house, but subsequently the Garden House was built at one end. It now looks on to a lawn, bounded at the far side by a lower wall with railings. The walls are of stone on the outside, brick inside, providing a setting for climbing and rambler roses, among them a 'Red Dorothy Perkins', a variety of clematis, a lovely honeysuckle and apple trees.

Commander Findlay has three chief horticultural loves—long, massed herbaceous borders; phloxes in every shade and large clumps of white flowers which contrast with the vivid colours of the borders. There are few rare or exotic specimens, but the whole concept is incomparable. Perhaps the most interesting plants are a *Clematis recta*, whose fragrant white star-shaped blossoms are followed by silky seedheads, and the yellow Turk's Head lily, *Lilium Szovitsianum*, grown from seed.

At the approach to the main border (one of several fine ones), a large veronica with long pale racemes provides a charming introduction to the delights to come.

This principal border measuring 100 yards by 4 yards lies opposite the Water Garden and is absolutely spectacular in high summer. There are delphiniums, gaillardias, heleniums, scabious, potentillas in vibrant reds, huge masses of loosestrife, giant filipendulas, yellow anthemis and a host of other favourites.

At the end of the Water Garden there is a good selection of astilbes, while irises, primulas and meconopses add their colour in spring. A delightful little summer-house contains two newly-repaired, black-painted Burmese figures of a man and a woman, as well as pieces of elaborately carved teak taken from the boats which collected the logs that had been floated down the Irrawaddy river to the delta.

Apart from the lime avenue, there are some fine old trees, among them a cut-leaf beech, *Fagus sylvatica heterophylla*. A long grassed walk, on both sides of which grows a fine and beautifully clipped (it had just been trimmed when we were there!) castellated yew hedge, leads to the walled garden.

It may come as a surprise to visitors that rhododendrons, azaleas and heaths do not feature at Carnell. The answer is simple—the soil is chalky and therefore anathema to ericaceous plants. When there is so much colour anyway throughout the seasons, this matters not a jot.

CAWDOR CASTLE, by Nairn

Owner: Earl of Cawdor

5 miles south of Nairn, by B9090

Daily from 1 April to 3 October
from 1000 hours to 1700 hours

Few places in Scotland, even in Britain, have stronger imaginative associations with the darker side of our ancient story than Cawdor Castle, according to legend first built on a site chosen by that beast of burden the ass, and commemorated to this day inside the present building by the bark of an ancient tree.

Shakespeare has made Cawdor (originally Calder) one of the most famous castles in Europe. The Calders of Calder were said to be descended from Macbeth's brother, to whom the king, on his assumption of the crown, resigned the Thanedom of Calder. The nucleus of the present spendid castle, the Tower of Calder, was built in 1454. The heiress Muriella Calder in 1510 married Sir John Campbell of Loch Awe, third son of the second Earl of Argyll (from whom the present line descends), whose descendant was created Baron Cawdor in 1796 and Earl of Cawdor in 1827. It will no doubt come as a surprise to many, as it did to us, that the stones of a stronghold so redolent with the violence of history—incidentally, singularly well captioned by the Earl himself—should also offer to its visitors one of the best-kept, most colourful and peaceful gardens in the Highlands.

There is a walled formal garden on the north side of the castle. Four large ovals with centre-pieces of roses occupy one section, beyond which, separated by a hedge, is a rose garden. There is also a magnificent herbaceous border, and a rose-covered pergola.

The walled garden leads into a wood through which nature trails ranging from a quarter of a mile to five miles may be followed. Here are located some magnificent mature trees. Apart from the usual broad-leafed species, there are clumps of rhododendrons, azaleas and bamboo. Western hemlock, *Tsuga heterophylla,* Wellingtonias, *Sequoiadendron giganteum,* single leaf ash, *Fraxinus excelsior diversifolia* and Nootka cyprus, *Chamaecyparis nootkatensis,* flourish among the ferns by the side of the peat-brown Cawdor Burn.

On the other side of the drawbridge entrance to the castle is a smaller walled garden which once contained a parterre, but at the moment of writing is closed for reconstruction. The park in which the castle is set is extensive.

While Cawdor Castle is itself of major interest, this well-maintained garden has considerable charm and should not be missed.

CLUNY HOUSE, Aberfeldy

Owners: Mr J and Mrs W Mattingley

3½ miles from Aberfeldy, off the Weem to Strathtay road, north of the River Tay

Daily 1 March to 30 October
from 1000 hours to 1800 hours

Cluny in Gaelic means 'the meadow place'. In front of the 1800 house (with additions dating from 1850) on a steep slope down towards the Tay, Mr and Mrs R S Masterton, who acquired the property in 1950, created one of Scotland's best plantsman's gardens. Mr and Mrs Mattingley, a daughter and son-in-law of the Mastertons, are continuing the development of the garden at Cluny.

A series of serpentine walks down through the woodland leads to small plots, screened from each other by trees and foliage, and every now and then to openings giving views of the hills and the river valley below.

The trees and shrubs include acers, birches, cherries and several species of rowans, *Sorbus*. Among these are many fine rhododendrons, magnolias, enkianthus, cotoneasters, viburnums, embothriums and eucryphias. Each of the months that the garden is open offers special attractions. Daffodils cover the lawns and other open spaces in spring, when the early rare primulas *edgeworthii, bhutanica* and *tanneri* come into bloom. May produces, besides the rhododendrons and magnolias, trilliums, clematis, meconopsis in a variety of shades of blue and yellow, berberis and lovely Candelabra primulas. Indeed, a former keeper of the Royal Botanic Gardens in Edinburgh once described Cluny as being 'a treasure-house of rare primulas'. Of these, the *petiolarids*, grown from seeds collected in the Himalayas and China, are of great interest. Another is the Himalayan *Primula sonchifolia* with its lavender-blue flowers. Gentians and nomocharis, from the high meadows of Western China, North Burma and southeast Tibet contrast with the Giant Lily, *Cardiocrinum giganteum*, on the verge of the wood. Notable, too, are the fiery tubular flowers of *Embothrium coccineum* and the white North American flowering dogwood *Cornus nuttallii*.

Some of the trees were chosen for their beautiful barks, for instance the Manchurian cherry and its Tibetan cousin, *Prunus serrula*. Others were selected for their brilliant fruits. Yet others were chosen, like the miniature Mountain ash, *Sorbus reducta*, the Spindle tree, *Euonymus*, and *Acer sieboldianum* for their magnificent autumnal display of foliage. *Disanthus cercidifolius*, *Cercidiphyllum japonicum*, enkianthus and *Eucryphia x nymansensis* as well add to a glorious palette of colour.

A new garden is in the process of being created on the Tyrolean-like grassy hillside behind the house.

Rhododendron 'HUMMINGBIRD'

COLZIUM-LENNOX ESTATE ARBORETUM and WALLED GARDEN

Owners: Cumbernauld and Kilsyth District Councils

Left past Kilsyth on A803 road from Glasgow

From the beginning of April until the last weekend of September from 1100 hours to 1900 hours daily

Of all the 'surprise' gardens in Scotland, none is more unexpected than that contained in the walled garden at Colzium. The site has absorbed plenty of history. There was once a Colzium Castle, only a fragment of which survives in the garden wall. It was put up prior to 1620 by the Livingstones of Callander (Falkirk), but was acquired by the Livingstones of Kilsyth, by which time the Callander Livingstones had become Earls of Linlithgow and Callander, ensconced in nearby Kilsyth Castle. Cromwell besieged and destroyed Kilsyth in 1650, though its owner was subsequently further ennobled for his royalist stance as Viscount Kilsyth and Baron Livingstone. Colzium Castle, however, escaped destruction. Viscount Kilsyth, while resigning the estate in favour of his younger brother, William, kept Colzium for himself. He was a fervent Jacobite and had to flee to Utrecht (Holland) in 1689. (Incidentally, his first wife was the widow of 'Bonnie Dundee'). In 1697 he returned to Scotland and for reasons which are unclear, pulled down Colzium. He died in Rome in 1755 without issue and the line of the Livingstones of Kilsyth came to an end.

The York Building Society (that opportunistic snapper-up of forfeited Jacobite estates) bought Colzium and leased it to the 'Tobacco Lord' Campbell of Shawfield, whose family later bought it and sold it (at a huge profit) to Sir Archibald Edmonston of Duntreath. It was he who built Colzium House in 1703. In 1930 the Edmonstons sold Colzium House to the Town Clerk of Kilsyth, Mr William MacKay Lennox, who, on his death in 1937, left the house and policies, some 68 acres, to the Burgh of Kilsyth. After being leased as a market garden during World War II, Kilsyth Burgh reacquired it in 1967 and in the early 1970s, in collaboration with the Countryside Commission for Scotland, drew up plans to rehabilitate and relandscape the southern portion of the estate. These works, begun in the spring of 1978, included the filling-in and levelling of the former market garden to the height of the rear of the slope, prior to laying out the present remarkable garden.

While some private owners of walled gardens are struggling to keep them in good trim, this one at Colzium is in magnificent heart, having the financial resources of the District Council to maintain it.

Some may level the criticism that it is a garden lacking in colour. Here you will find no herbaceous borders ablaze with every rainbow hue, but rather the interest is provided by a huge and varied collection of shrubs and trees of every shape, height and texture, from the conical conifers to the large spreading leaves of the Indian Bean Tree, *Catalpa bignonioides*, whose leaves emit a pungent odour when crushed. It is virtually impossible to imagine such a glorious variety of greens. There are the luminous yellow-greens of *Berberis aurea* and *Jasminum parkeri aureum*; the dark shades of the various cypresses and the subtle grey-blue of the spruce, 'Sanders Blue', and the Scaly juniper, *Juniperus squamata* 'Blue Star'. Indeed, the colours in this garden are all subtle and merge beautifully together. A violet-pink abelia blends with the purple of two dwarf rhododendrons, a form of *saluenense*, and *russatum* 'Keillour', as well as with the berberises, 'Dart's Red Lady' and *thunbergii atropurpurea* 'Nana'. Colzium contains a wide variety of berberises, such as 'Silver Beauty', 'Rose Glow' and 'Bagatelle' among others. A *Cotinus* 'Royal Purple' startles the eye with the strength of its colour.

The high walls which surround the garden are clothed with golden hop, solanum, *Hydrangea petiolaris* and the lovely *Desfontainea spinosa* 'Harold Comber', whose bright red trumpets light up the more sombre greens of the other climbers, as do the pale pink bells of a gaultheria and the tiny tubes of a *Penstemon pinifolius* in other beds.

It is impossible in such a short space to mention more than a few of the plants in this remarkable garden. The heavily mulched ground in spring hosts crocuses, snowdrops, cyclamen (the delightful pale pink *inti-*

minata form is a miniature treasure in high summer) and other seasonal delights. One specimen which must be mentioned, however, is the unusual Gutta Percha Tree, not often seen in Scotland.

Among the most rewarding features of Colzium is the meticulous naming of every plant, including in many instances the common name as well as the Latin. Just two examples are the Sowbread (cyclamen) and Cowberry (*Vaccinium vitis-idaea*).

Immediately outside the garden, there are fairly recent plantings including the Bearberry, *Arctostaphylos uva-ursi,* whose racemes of white, flushed pink, urn-shaped flowers are followed by red globose berries. There is also a *Magnolia campbellii mollicomata* 'Lanarth' which in time will illumine this part of what is an outstanding garden and one that should be lingered in for many hours.

The policies include a curling pond, well-maintained and re-planted woodland walks above the Colzium burn—an arboretum is in process of development—the Clock Tower Theatre, restored from the former dairy buildings, and an excavated Ice House originally dating from the 17th century though repaired for re-use during the 19th century.

Catalpa bignonioides

CRARAE GARDENS, by Inveraray

Owner: The Crarae Gardens Charitable Trust

On A83, just past Furnace, midway between Inveraray and Lochgilphead

Summer, from 0900 hours to 1800 hours;
Winter, daylight hours

Once the estate was part of the great Lordship of Glassary, owned by the Macgilliechrists, until marriage to a Scrymgeour from Angus brought the lands to that family. In 1688, as a result of the politico-religious troubles of the times, it was granted to the 3rd Earl of Lauderdale, who retained the superiority until 1718, when the lands of Glassary were acquired by Sir James Campbell of Auchinleck, who sold them to his kinsman, Dugald Campbell of Ederline. He, however, got so heavily into debt that the estate had to be sold off in lots. Lot 3, about 6000 acres, was sold to John Tait of Harvieston in Clackmannan, who renamed his purchase after his wife's Galloway estate, Cumlodden. Tait's son sold it in 1825 to his brother-in-law, Sir Archibald Campbell of Succoth, the 2nd Baronet, whose great-great-great grandson is the present laird.

The garden is laid out around the steep glen through which the Crarae Burn tumbles down to Loch Fyne. It is generally believed that in 1800 Tait planted the European larch and Scots pine, taken from remnants of the Caledonian forest, and which now sweep west-wards across the burn. Because the Campbells' principal home was at Garscube, near Glasgow, Cumlodden was more or less a summer residence. When there, they stayed in what is now Goatfield Farm, then an inn, until 1893, when Lady Campbell, widow of the 4th Baronet, pulled down the inn and erected the present house. Only a single *Cupressus lawsoniana* survives from the rose garden she created. She died in 1904 and Sir Archibald Campbell, the 5th Baronet, heired the estate. His wife was a keen gardener and an aunt of the famous plant collector, Reginald Farrer. While her rock garden north-west of the house has disappeared, the two curved shrub borders to the east of it survive. They include the splendid *Eucryphia cordifolia, Osmanthus delavayi, Osmarea burkwoodii* and *Cercidiphyllum japonicum.* She also planted two *Eucalyptus urnigera* given to her by Farrer which, though badly damaged, managed to survive the gale of 15 January 1968, and are now sending out new shoots. Around and among Tait's larches, she also introduced several rhododendrons, among the most spectacular being *R falconeri.*

The making of the present glen garden really began in 1925 when Sir Archibald handed over the estate to his son, later Sir George Campbell. Sir George had long been interested in trees. As a lad of 14, he brought by governess cart from Inveraray Castle a Silver fir, *Abies grandis,* now 102 feet high. In 1917, while a young officer stationed in Edinburgh, he visited Dawyck, the home of R S Balfour, who gave him a *Cunninghamia lanceolata* in a pot, remarking, 'I can't grow this thing here. You'd better take it to Crarae. It might grow there.' Today, it is over 50 feet high.

While Sir George did not subscribe to the plant-hunting expeditions of his time, many of his friends did, and sent him their surplus seedlings and seeds. Gifts also came from many other sources, resulting in today's glorious autumn display of sorbus, acer, prunus, cotoneaster and berberis. Sir George had no overall design intention, but a wonderful eye for finding the right setting for a particular planting; as, for example, his placing of *Disanthus cercidifolius* so that, in James Truscott's words, 'its cascading scarlet autumn foliage "mirrors" the movement of the waterfall next to it', or the positioning of the Chinese *Hydrangea aspera* by the footbridge which traverses the top of the glen.

During the 1950s, Mr Michael Noble, later Lord Glenkinglas, began to cross selected species and hybrids to try to achieve a bright red rhododendron flower throughout the season. Seed from some of these crosses was germinated at Crarae and the plants massed in a single colourful area. Two of the clones have been registered: one named 'Secretary of State', Lord Glenkinglas being Secretary of State for Scotland in that year; the other, 'Shadow Secretary', he by then being no longer in office.

In 1967, Sir George died and his son, Sir Ilay, took over and has continued the garden's development. To ensure its future, in 1978 Sir Ilay made the gardens over to a Charitable Trust, which is seeking to create an endowment fund.

The tour of this splendid gorge garden, now over 50 acres, is necessarily a lengthy and somewhat strenuous affair, even if the inner circle walk (taking a robust walker 45 minutes) is chosen rather than the outer (at a conservative estimate, two hours). Both routes begin and end at the carpark. There is generous provision of seats, supplying convenient rest points as well as affording several spectacular views over Loch Fyne. Visitors will be rewarded by snowdrops, daffodils and bluebells in season; a primula dell flowering beneath a eucalyptus canopy; a wide variety of magnolias, azaleas and rhododendrons, including *R fulvum, R hodgsonii, R arizelum* and *R bureavii*. But it is primarily the shrubs and trees that lend the garden its October glory—the Chinese beech, *Fagus engleriana*; the sorbus, 'Joseph Rock'; several eucryphia, including the Irish-raised *E* '*Mr Usher*' and *E lucida* and the ornamental Crab apple, *Malus hupehensis*. There are some Southern beeches, *Nothofagus*, and a Monkey Puzzle, *Araucaria araucana*, once popular, if not so long-lived as this one, in many a Clyde coast garden. There is also a fine red-barked Strawberry Tree, *Arbutus menziesii*.

Maintained by only three people, this is a garden to be visited in spring and again in autumn. It is greatly to be hoped that the Charitable Trust's endeavours to raise an endowment fund of £250 000 can speedily be realized, or the future of this great Argyll garden could be in jeopardy.

CRATHES CASTLE, Banchory

Owner: The National Trust for Scotland

5 miles east of Banchory, off A93

1 April to 31 October from 1100 hours to 1800 hours. Other times by appointment only

The Anglo-Saxon Burnards, or Burnetts, came to Scotland along with many other Norman and English families (including the Norman Lindsays) during the reign of David I. Alexander Burnard (a follower of Robert the Bruce) had his services rewarded with the gift of an estate at Banchory and the position of Royal Forester of nearby Drum. As his badge of office, he is said to have received the decorated ivory 'Horn of Leys', still in Crathes Castle. For the next two and a half centuries the Burnetts made their home in a fort on the Loch of Leys, until in 1529 Alexander Burnett, following his marriage to a canon's daughter, began to build Crathes Castle, an exercise which, in troublous times, took 40 years. Thus it was his grandson, also Alexander, who moved into the completed castle in 1578. His son, Sir Thomas, became the first Baronet. The line lasted in Scotland until General Sir James Burnett of Leys, one of whose sons died before him, the other having been killed in action in 1945. The title therefore passed to Sir Alexander William Burnett Ramsay, who lives in new South Wales, while General Sir James's daughter became heir to the Scottish estate. The General made over the castle and part of the estate to the National Trust for Scotland, whose hands it came into in 1952.

It is perhaps worth noting that this distinguished family, besides providing soldiers, sailors and governors of American states, also produced Bishop Gilbert Burnett of Salisbury Cathedral, author of an eminently readable diary, and that eccentric Scottish judge Lord Monboddo who, anticipating Darwin, believed that babies were born with tails, immediately cut off by a conspiracy of midwives.

There was a garden at Crathes when it was visited in the days of the 11th Baronet, Sir Robert Burnett of Leys, by Gertrude Jekyll around 1895, because she includes an illustration of it in her book *Colour Schemes for the*

Flower Garden. In its present form, however, this exquisite garden is the work of Sir James and Lady Sybil, the last resident Baronet and his wife. They were both practical gardeners, he with a wide knowledge of trees and shrubs; she with a rare eye for colour combinations and a special interest in herbaceous plants.

The whole garden is made up of eight small gardens, each with its own thematic characteristic. The four on an upper level are divided by a large Aviary border and by the wall against which lean the Mackenzie and Moncur greenhouses, rebuilt in 1978 by a local contractor to the original design. They are enclosed by a yew hedge, one side of which is believed to have been planted in 1702.

The entrance leads to the White Border which has as its centrepiece a Portugal laurel, *Prunus lusitanica*. To the left is the Camel Garden, where may be found *Decaisnea fargesii*, *Prunus subhirtella* 'Autumnalis Rosea', *Agapanthus* 'Headbourne hybrids' and *Trillium grandiflorum*. On the other side of the White Border is the Golden Garden, developed since 1973 on the site of the former nursery, now moved to a site in the vegetable garden. It had been Lady Burnett's intention to create such a garden, following the suggestion in Gertrude Jekyll's book, but she did not live to carry out her plans fully. Help in its making was given by her friend and confidante, the late Frances Chenevix Trench, and of course by the Head Gardener, Douglas MacDonald. Here may be found *Viburnum opulus* 'Xanthocarpum', *Malus* 'Golden Hornet', *Philadelphus coronarius* 'Aureus', *Weigela* 'Loovmansii Aurea', *Taxus baccata* 'Fastigiata Aurea', *Rosa* 'Agnes' and *Humulus lupulus* 'Aureus', among many other interesting plants. The Golden Garden is separated from the Red Garden by the June Border created in 1945, at the end of which the dovecot provides an eye-stop, moved in 1937 to its present site for this very purpose. A brilliant display of colour, this section features lupins, bearded iris in glorious shades, several varieties of oriental poppies and pyrethrums, as well as other lovely things in typical cottage garden style.

The triangular Red Garden contains among its treasures *Lonicera ledebourii*, *Potentilla* 'Red Ace', *Rosa*

'Frensham', *Euphorbia griffithii* 'Fireglow', *Buddleia davidii* 'Royal Red', *Corylus maxima* 'Purpurea', *Berberis thunbergii* 'Red Chief' and *Weigela florida* 'Foliis purpureis'. The other triangle behind the June Border is now used to bring on plants.

Across the White Border, beneath the Camel Garden, is the Trough Garden with, notably, *Prunus serrula, Acer griseum, Virburnum x juddii* and *Syringa yunnanensis.*

The upper four gardens above the Aviary Border contain the croquet lawn, leading to the Upper Pool Garden, the last to be devised by Lady Burnett and finished in 1932. The dominant colours here are yellow, red and bronze, *Coreopsis verticillata* contrasting with the bronze-leaved bugle. Here may also be found *Schizophragma integrifolium, Buddleia colvillei, Lonicera splendida, Clematoclethra integrifolia, Rosa* 'Veilchenblau' and *Schisandra rubriflora.*

Down the steps in the middle of the yew border is the Fountain or Blue Garden, bedded out with plants, obviously, in various shades of blue. The fountained statue in the centre of the pool is a replica of a Florentine statue once to be seen in Florence's Palazzo Vecchio.

The remaining upper garden is the Rose Garden, laid out as four approximately triangular beds, containing mostly differently coloured floribundas. There is also a Handkerchief tree, *Davidia involucrata,* a group of Crab apples, *Malus* 'John Downie', and around its base a curious pink dandelion, *Crepis incana.*

The main double herbaceous border is a further delight. The greenhouses, with their wide variety of fuchsias and a sheer wall of red geraniums, are also remarkable. They contain in addition a splendid collection of rare Malmaison carnations.

It is impossible fully to describe the richness and incomparable variety of Crathes Garden, or to convey the subtlety of its design in such a brief summary as this. Along with Inverewe in Rosshire, very different in character, Crathes undoubtedly takes a leading place as one of the twin garden glories in the great heritage held and managed by the National Trust for Scotland.

Surrounding the gardens are 595 acres of the Crathes Estate; delightful woodland scenery, including some magnificent and very old trees (one or two dating from 1860) and a variety of trails — 15 miles in all including the 6½ miles of the Ley Way Trail and a short one for the disabled.

CULZEAN CASTLE AND COUNTRY PARK, Ayrshire

Owner: The National Trust for Scotland (who maintain the gardens and policies for the Country Park Joint Committee)

11 miles south of Ayr, on A719

Gardens and park all year round from 0900 hours to dusk; castle and other services daily from 1 April to 31 October from 1030 hours to 1730 hours

The present Culzean Castle was built by Robert Adam over the period 1777–92 (replacing the previous large tower house with extensive outbuildings on the clifftop) for David, 10th Earl of Cassillis. It is a huge but elegant Palladian-style building with a particularly fine oval staircase and numerous ancillary buildings, now admirably converted to provide a restaurant, shop, offices and other services required for the country park.

The 12th Earl of Cassillis was created Marquess of Ailsa in 1831. In 1945, the 5th Marquess of Ailsa, 16th Earl of Cassillis, gave Culzean to the National Trust for Scotland. The policy lands, together covering 530 acres, contain woodland, some of which has been given over to commercial forestry under the pressure of economic circumstances; but many splendid trees of great antiquity and size have been carefully preserved.

The gardens fall into three main sections, if one can use such a word in the context of so vast a scale of things. Beneath the terrace in front of the castle is a formally designed sunken garden, with a statue-fountain in a pool as its centrepiece. According to Sir Herbert Maxwell, writing in *Scottish Gardens* (1908), this 'natural gully, originally deepened for defensive purposes, has been cast into a couple of walled terraces forming a delectable abode for many shrubs which cannot face an inland winter. The peculiar conformation of the ground affords that shelter from blustering winds and salt-laden gales which so often neutralise the genial influence of the sea-side.' At that time, Maxwell observed that 'the terraces, so ample in their proportions, so admirably suited in their south-easterly aspect for the culture of rare exotics, have not yet been turned to full account, as doubtless they soon will be, for their owner, the

Marquess of Ailsa, constantly resides in the home of his ancestors, and is an enthusiastic and skilful amateur.' There is nothing amateurish about the approach of the National Trust for Scotland where the tending of great gardens is concerned. The east-facing herbaceous border on the terrace is bright with golden and bronze alstroemeria, *Phygelius capensis* and other traditional perennials.

Particularly striking is the border facing the castle, with a magnificent display of red and pink astilbes reaching its entire length, the intensity of their complementary colours emphasizing the sheer scale of the border. At Culzean, everything is on a grand scale.

The sunken Fountain Garden is reached by steps set in four miniature towers on two levels along the walls. The lower border, the walls of which are hung with clematis and climbing roses, is bright with colour supplied by, amongst other plants, *Anthemis tinctoria* 'E C Burton', a splendid acanthus and a remarkable, towering *Echium peninana*, a monocarpic native of the Canary Isles. On the other side of the path, plots punctuated with Cordyline palms contain *Kniphofia caulescens*, the Red Hot Poker, as does another border running the full length of the lawn.

This long lawn once carried two tennis courts, but these have long since been smoothly grassed over. At the south side of the Fountain Garden, there is a large orangery, outside of which dieramas nod their heads. Inside, it is given over to figs, abutilons, strelitzias and oleanders, as well as, of course, pots of oranges.

The walled garden lies a quarter of a mile or so away to the south, and has also been laid out in the grand manner. Fruit and vegetables are grown, together with a spectacularly colourful and lovely double herbaceous border. A centrally dividing wall separates this section from the rose garden, rich in old-fashioned shrub varieties and with two more floral borders. A multi-faceted sundial, telling the time in various places, stands on the grass path down the central double herbaceous border. Here, too, are the glasshouses and the plant-selling area.

It is possible to drive round much of the estate. Its three main sections each has an individual car park, although there is also a network of pedestrian paths.

Throughout the richly wooded policies there are rare trees, many of them of considerable age. Culzean also contains about 40 small architectural 'features', including a power house, an ice house, a hillside camellia house and a viaduct.

So varied, indeed, are the facilities, and so rewarding, that with the exception of the 18th-century 'model' industrial village of New Lanark, Culzean draws more visitors annually than any other rural non-Government-owned heritage site in Scotland.

DAWYCK BOTANIC GARDEN, Stobo

Owner: Royal Botanic Garden Edinburgh

1 mile from Stobo, 8 miles south-west of Peebles on the B720 road

Daily from 15 March to 22 October from 1000 hours to 1800 hours and at other times by special arrangement

The Veitch family owned Dawyck from the 13th to the late 17th century. Little is known about them, although they were hosts to James IV when Dawyck's herons provided quarry for the king's falcons. To protect their property from the cold winds, the family surrounded it with plantations of trees.

The estate was acquired in 1691 by Sir James Naesmyth, a lawyer whose practices led to his being dubbed 'the Deil o' Dawyck'. He was, however, a keen gardener, introducing new species from Europe and North America. His grandson, also Sir James, was a pupil of the famous Swedish botanist Carl Linnaeus, who was responsible for the first scientific naming of plants. This Sir James improved his policies by planting an avenue of *Abies alba,* European Silver firs. He passed on his enthusiasm to his heirs and successors, one of whom, Sir James Murray Naesmyth, commissioned the architect William Burn to design a new house, which was completed in 1832. He employed a team of Italian craftsmen to set out the striking terraces, steps, bridges and urns that are a major feature of the landscape.

Sir James's interest in trees led him to subscribe to the great overseas plant-hunts of the middle 19th century, including David Douglas's north-west American expedition which produced so many magnificent conifers. He also planted some 800 hectares of mixed woodland, including Scots pine grown from seed collected in the remains of the Caledonian forest, near Braemar. Dawyck's most famous tree, however, is probably the Fastigiate beech, *Fagus sylvatica* 'Dawyck', discovered by Sir James among ordinary beeches and removed to the south side of the house, where it has now reached a height of over 70 feet.

In 1897, the estate became the property of the Balfour family. The creator of the garden in its present form,

F R S Balfour, was himself an enthusiastic foreign-plant collector, bringing back from north-west America many conifers for the arboretum, as well as a wide range of flowering shrubs, including 120 or so hardy rhododendrons, which, unlike some other imported plants, mostly survived the frosts and roaring winds, secure in the garden's moist leaf mould. In 1908, he found Brewer's Weeping spruce, *Picea breweriana,* which he later imported. The E H Wilson 1907 expedition to China brought back seed of *Prunus x dawyckensis.* Another Chinese import is the holly, *Ilex fargesii,* still flourishing beside the bridge over the Scrape Burn, a tributary of the River Tweed, which runs through the grounds.

In 1978, F R S Balfour's son, Colonel Alastair Balfour, gifted the estate to the nation. Cleared, restored and replanted, it now plays its part in the educational and research work of Scotland's national Botanic Garden, the Royal Botanic Garden Edinburgh. A visit to Dawyck is a 'must' for anyone considering planting a wood.

While the estate is dominated by its range of conifers, there is a formal azalea terrace on the lower slopes of Chapel Hill. This crossed, the beauty of the Scrape Glen lies before the visitor. A series of walks traverses the hill on either side of Scrape Burn, over which the Swiss bridge is a striking feature. In addition, there is a walled garden with an Italian wellhead, the picturesque red-roofed chapel of Dawyck, now the lairds' mausoleum, and in spring spectacular carpets of daffodils and snowdrops. In the woodland clearings trilliums and Himalayan poppies flourish.

DRUM CASTLE, Aberdeenshire

Owner: The National Trust for Scotland

Off A93 Aberdeen to Banchory road

Garden of Historic Roses from 1 May to 31 October, daily from 1000 hours to 1800 hours. Grounds daily, all year from 0930 hours to sunset. For castle opening hours apply to the National Trust for Scotland

Drum Castle, on Royal Deeside, was the home of the Irvine family for 653 years. William de Irwin had been a loyal follower of King Robert the Bruce, and was rewarded with the estate of Drum, then a royal hunting forest. The 4th Laird played some part in negotiating the release of the poet-king James I of Scotland, who had been captured by the English as a boy and held by them for 18 years. The Jacobean mansion was added to the 300-year-old tower of Drum in 1619 by the 9th Laird. The 14th Laird fought for the Old Pretender at Sheriffmuir in 1715, being wounded so severely in the head that he died insane. The 17th Laird fought for Prince Charles Edward Stuart. He took part in the Battle of Culloden, but managed to escape. His head gardener, who had fought with him, also escaped, and was reported to have made a fortune collecting horseshoe nails and other booty from the battlefield. The house was Victorianized by David Bryce. The 24th and last Laird of Drum entered into an agreement with the National Trust for Scotland whereby Drum, with its 411 acres, would be held for the benefit of the nation.

Most of the grounds of Drum were developed by the Irvines (or Forbes Irvines, as they became) as landscape with interesting trees, among them a Handkerchief tree, *Davidia involucrata,* first introduced to Britain from west China by Ernest Wilson in 1869. He introduced as well the large-leaved *Populus lasiocarpa* that is also in the grounds. At the west end of the lawn there is an American chestnut, *Aesculus flava.* The many fine conifers include the lovely Brewer's Weeping spruce, *Picea breweriana,* from Chile, and such native-by-adoption specimens as the Douglas fir, *Pseudotsuga menziesii,* by the gate of the walled garden.

There is a broad green sward which leads down to the

82

walled garden, where the splendid collection of historic and modern roses is to be found. Among a great many other varieties, there are examples of 'Fantin-Latour', the 'Rosemary Rose', 'Sally Holmes' and the lovely shrimp-pink *Rosa* 'Nevada', a modern shrub. Roses clamber up fences interspersed with interesting forms of clematis, such as 'Dorothy Walton', 'Rambling Rector' and 'Royal Velours'. Climbing up the long walls there is a yellow *Clematis orientalis* 'Orange Peel' as well as *Aristolochia macrophylla*, the Dutchman's Pipe, and *Vitis coignetiae*, the Japanese crimson glory vine.

This formal section has been laid out with geometric beds, which contain a mixture of roses and herbaceous plants. Three of the plots have been given over to the type of garden popular in the 18th, 19th and 20th centuries, and contain flowers which are typical of these periods. There is also a central circular paved area where the unusual sundial and its months are set in colourful mosaic patterns.

The pond, situated on the left as one approaches the walled garden, is an area of tranquillity where ducks dabble. Here the customary water-loving plants surround it.

North-west of the estate are the 117 acres of the Old Forest of Drum, one of the last remnants of a vast forest that once covered the lower slopes of the Dee Valley. In this part of the estate oak, Scots pine and birch prevail, although among other interesting species there are some ancient gnarled cherry trees.

DRUMMOND CASTLE, Muthill

Owner: Grimethorpe and Drummond Castle Trust

3 miles south of Crieff, on the A822 Muthill to Crieff road

Daily from 1400 hours to 1800 hours
from May to September

Drummond Castle was built on a rocky outcrop by John, 1st Lord Drumond. The 4th Lord Drummond accompanied the Earl of Nottingham to Spain in 1605 to secure a peace treaty, for which service Lord Drummond was created 1st Earl of Perth by James VI and I. His brother, the 2nd Earl, a Privy Councillor to James VI and Charles I, succeeded in 1612 and is credited with transforming both the gardens — he was much influenced by gardens he had seen in France — and the castle. He had the 3rd John Mylne, of the famous Mylne family who built for several generations of royalty, design a Renaissance-style block to the south of the keep. Mylne was also responsible for the unusual obelisk sundial, the centrepiece of the garden, the 50 faces of which told the time in most of Europe's capital cities. The keep still stands (as does the sundial, though its faces are now badly worn), but the rest of the castle was restored and largely remodelled by the 1st Earl of Ancaster in 1890.

The gardens have thus a long history, having supplied cherries for James IV in 1508 when that monarch was hunting in the Glen Artney Forest. The garden was probably already of some significance in 1630, since Mylne's sundial was put in position in that year.

The Perths were dedicated Royalists. The Duke of Perth, 'out' in the rising of 1715, apparently returned from that adventure to a garden 'full of evergreens and flowers', in which there were 'water-works' (as there still are). His involvement in the 1745 rising, however, was more disastrous. After the Jacobite defeat at Culloden in 1746, the Duke died on board a ship on its way to France and the estates were attainted. They were not regained until 1785. The lake that now adorns the park was created on the site where the pacifying military lived in a fortified 'village'.

The estate was surveyed for military purposes between 1747 and 1755 by General Roy, providing the first certain evidence of the existence of a formal garden — 'four grass platts or plots symmetrically arranged on the plain below the castle, with a broad central avenue extending southwards from the garden and across the site of the present kitchen garden'. The scale of Roy's survey was too small to show any terracing, but this appears in the next survey, that carried out in 1810 by James Knox, by which time the kitchen garden had been restocked and much new woodland planting carried out. The taste of the times, however, precluded the restoration of the original formal garden.

Early in the 19th century, both the parterre and the formal terracing in front of the castle were re-established, principally the work of Lewis Kennedy, gardener son of a well-known botanist, John Kennedy, a partner in the Vineyard Nursery at Hammersmith which, in the late 18th and early 19th centuries, supplied plants to many of the finest gardens in Britain. Lewis became factor to the Drummond Estates in 1818 after a long career as a landscape gardener, partly at Malmaison, France, in the employment of the Empress Josephine. Under Kennedy, between 1818 and 1868, when he retired, the Drummond estate became extremely profitable. His greatest achievement, however, was possibly his creation of the formal flower garden at Drummond.

The architect Sir Charles Barry exhibited a series of drawings for the redesigning of the castle at the Royal Academy in London in 1828. Fortunately, perhaps, they were never implemented. The terracing, however, possibly reveals his influence, being similar in design, though more elegant, than that in front of Dunrobin Castle, where he was certainly active. The Drummond Castle terracing has been replanted with a wide range of well-maintained shrubs, and includes yuccas, although these do not always take kindly to the frosts of a Scottish winter. Lewis's son, G P Kennedy, who was Barry's pupil and who in turn became the Drummond factor and agent, was responsible for the redesigning of the parterre about 1838.

Thus when Queen Victoria visited Drummond Castle in 1842, she and Prince Albert 'walked in the garden which is really very fine, with terraces, like an old French garden' (though to our eyes today, as the contemporary painting by Jacob Thomson confirms, it would probably have looked horribly cluttered). Today, when the visitor walks across the courtyard beyond the entrance gateway and comes out upon the balcony at the top of the terrace steps, the first impact the garden makes is tremendous. Ahead runs the central north–south axis, leading through a classical arch at the far end of the garden, to a green swathe running through woodland to the summit of the opposite hill. Drawing the countryside into the garden is, of course, a French idea; but the garden itself is Italian in inspiration, with statuary, possibly brought from Italy by Barry in the 1830s, fountains and terracing, as well as urns from the Abercorn pottery in Portobello, also manufactured in the 1830s. By later Victorian times, indeed, the garden had become something of a clutter, the paths being lined with 'sparkling spar', which upset Gertrude Jekyll when she visited Drummond in 1918.

As might have been expected, the garden suffered neglect during both World Wars. It was Phyllis Astor, wife of the 3rd Earl of Ancaster, who decided to restore the garden after World War II, removing the offending path-linings and relieving the clutter. Many of the former features were retained, including the ancient yew hedges at either end of the terracing and paths, and the two, now huge, Copper beech trees planted to commemorate Queen Victoria's visit. The structure of the parterre has also been preserved, the Victorian box-edged borders along the diagonal grass walks presently containing white-flowered, silver-leafed *Anaphalis triplinervis,* and the central cross-walks lavender edgings.

The main feature of the garden is the box-hedge parterre segmented to resemble the Saltire, or St Andrew's cross, the plots being filled with hybrid pink and yellow roses. At either end are two circular parterres each with a statue in the middle of a pond played on by fountains. Here, the plots are filled with 'Iceberg' roses.

Although Lady Ancaster's restoration did involve some thinning of the shrubbery, many ornamental trees remain, including Japanese maples; the Fastigiate Golden elm, *Ulmus x hollandica* 'Wredei'; two striking Purple oaks, *Quercus petraea* 'Purpurea'; fine specimens of *Acer pseudoplatanus* 'Prinz Handjery', and twinned pairs of *Prunus cerasifera* 'Pissardii'. The conical clipped trees are English and Irish yews and hollies.

The visitors' approach to the gardens from the Muthill to Crieff road is through a long avenue lined with venerable beeches. The ornamental lake lies to the right. The way out leads through a broad expanse of rolling parkland. In order that castle, gardens and parkland should be conserved for the enjoyment of future generations, the family set up the Grimethorpe and Drummond Castle Trust in the 1970s.

DUNROBIN CASTLE, Golspie, Sutherland

Owner: The Sutherland Trust

1 mile north of Golspie on A9

May: Monday to Thursday from 1030 hours to 1230 hours
June–September: Monday to Saturday from 1030 hours to
1730 hours; Sunday from 1300 hours to 1730 hours; 1–15
October: Monday to Saturday from 1030 hours to 1630 hours;
Sunday from 1300 hours to 1630 hours

Dunrobin Castle claims to be the oldest inhabited house in Scotland, a claim which would certainly be challenged by Traquhair House in the Borders. Dunrobin dates in part from the 13th century and with its 189 rooms it is certainly the largest house in the Highlands. Additions were made about 1650 and 1780 but the castle as it now stands is largely the work of Sir Charles Barry, architect of the Houses of Parliament in London, built in 1845.

The 2nd Duke and his Duchess had been first attracted by the gardens which Barry had designed in the French manner for the great houses of Harewood in Yorkshire and Cliveden in Berkshire. Barry, like others, had been much influenced by the gardens at Versailles.

The gardens at Dunrobin, reached by flights of steps, were laid out in 1848–9 by Barry. Protected on both sides by woodland, they form a high-walled enclosure. They are best appreciated from the balustrade which runs the length of the seaward facade of the castle: a large circular parterre on the left side and two rectangular parterres on the right.

The northern parterre, punctuated by yew trees, laurel and holly and the four corners, consists of four 'W'-shaped sections marked out by box hedging. The plots have recently been replanted with potentilla and lavender. Eight clipped cone-shaped yews of various heights stand near the centre, while closer to the middle are four Japanese angelica trees, *Aralia elata*. The central fountain, in the words of James Truscott, 'adds a baroque flourish to a scene which, with the silhouette of the chateau-style castle in the background, creates the illusion that a slice of the Loire Valley has been unexpectedly transplanted to the Scottish shore'. They are, of course, the most northerly sizeable gardens in these islands, being only two degrees south of St Petersburg and Greenland.

A background, mounded shrub border contains weigela, a large *Mahonia japonica*, escallonia, Candelabra primulas and an *Olearia macrodonta*.

The main axis leads to graceful wrought-iron gates in the east wall, gifted by the 1st Duke of Westminster in 1894, opening on to a private pier on the shore of the Dornoch Firth.

To the south is the other formal garden, divided into two by a mound of laurel, yew, holly and hebe. Two low box-edged rectangles have a central pool with a fountain in the middle, the plots having varieties of *Geranium sanguineum*.

There are three fine herbaceous borders, two of them down either side of the central walk to the Westminster gates. These contain traditional perennials and a charming *Asphodelus luteus*. To the front of them, colour is provided by low-growing aubretia, dianthus, catmint and saxifrage.

The main herbaceous border lies under the castle wall. Here there is a profusion of delphiniums, monkshood, foxgloves (that wild plant which nevertheless fits so well into many a Scottish garden) and several vigorous fuchsias. The Globe thistle, *Echinops vitro*, buddleias, paeonies and poppies add colour and contrast to a brilliant display. Roses climb up the wall behind interspersed with apple trees, a survival perhaps of what Sir Robert Gooden recalled seeing in these gardens—'fair orchards and gardens planted with all kyndes of fruits, hearbs, and floores used in this kingdom'.

To the north of the house there are extensive woodland walks.

EARLSHALL

Owners: The Baron and Baroness of Earlshall
1 mile from Leuchars on A919
June to September (closed Tuesdays)

The lands of Earlshall were granted to Sir William Bruce by charter from James IV in 1497. Bruce survived Flodden and in 1546 began the building of the present castle. His grandson, Andrew 'Bloody' Bruce, was second-in-command to Graham of Claverhouse. In the later part of the 18th century, the property was owned by the Bruce Hendersons until sold to Colonel Samuel Long, a Kentishman, in 1824. He never lived there and it remained unoccupied until 1891, falling into a state of disrepair although still roofed. In that year it was bought by Robert Mackenzie, a bleach merchant from Dundee, who gave the task of restoring both castle and the abandoned garden to Robert Lorimer (later Sir Robert). A contemporary of Gertrude Jekyll and Sir Edwin Lutyens, Lorimer knew them both and was influenced by their ideas.

On the death of his first wife, Jessie, Mackenzie sold Earlshall in 1926 to Sir Michael Nairn, of the Kirkcaldy linoleum firm. Sir Michael gave it to his daughter, Rachel, on her marriage to Arthur Purvis. Mrs Purvis died a widow in 1981. Two years later, the Baron and Baroness of Earlshall moved in. One of the Baron's Baxter ancestors fought for Prince Charles Edward Stuart, was captured and in 1746 departed to Barbados. The Baron and Baroness are both related to the first Sir William Bruce.

On one side, 14 acres of parkland still reach up to the walls of the castle. On the other, as Lorimer noted in his original survey, 'You stroll into the garden enclosed, but what a promise can such a place be! Such surprises — little gardens within the garden!'

The cobbled courtyard from where a tour of the garden begins is brightened by geraniums in troughs, alpines, orange-blossom and honeysuckle. It lies between the castle wall and the two-storey 'Dummy Daws', named after a dumb 18th-century coachman. It has a finely carved stone monkey on the roof. A flagged path leads to the topiary garden, for which Earlshall is principally famous.

The topiary yews, 36 in all, were transplanted from a disused Edinburgh garden when they were already mature. Lorimer, it is said, offered £5 for each of the trees successfully established at Earlshall. All survived the move, earning the head gardener £180, a large sum of money in those days.

Overlooked by a huge lime tree, the yews represent symbolic chess pieces, though some are shaped like abstract birds. Viewed from one of the upper windows of the castle, it can be seen that they are set out in the form of four saltires. The chess pieces begin to look a little ragged by the end of the season, when they have to be reclipped.

On the far side of this topiary display, Lorimer erected an arch bearing the Shakespearian inscription — 'Here shall ye see no enemy but winter and rough weather' — from *As You Like It*. The arch leads to a wooded shelter-belt, which takes some of the force out of the North Sea winds. On the other side of the gateway is the legend 'Who loves a garden still keeps his Eden'.

Clipped walls of yew and holly divide 'the gardens within the garden', or rooms, as the Baroness calls them. An east–west alley of yew trees runs along the outside of the topiary garden. At the far end is a stone arbour with slate-topped pillars marking its junction with the wall on either side. There is a sheltered stone seat and a sundial, which stands in a scented setting of Tea and Floribunda roses. Alcoves along the grassy yew alley house fuchsias, *Rosa fragrantissima* and azaleas.

At the west end, immediately behind 'Dummy Daws' and through a holly arch, is the 'secret garden', so called because one comes upon it unexpectedly. This was once a pond, but it has been filled in, and through its irregular slabs grow geraniums, love-in-the-mist, lewisia and white jasmine. In a walled corner there are climbing hydrangeas, camellias, roses and Lamb's Ear.

The orchard garden is reached through an arch in the hedge. It is enclosed on two sides by the wall surrounding the vegetable garden. In the centre is a stone plinth covered in honeysuckle. Round the plinth are some very old apple trees, the blossom of which adds spring colour to the spread of daffodils beneath. Asters, marigolds and cornflowers, together with herbaceous perennials along the walls, provide the colours of summer.

The orchard garden leads to the rose terrace and a large lawn known as the 'bowling green', although the game is thought never to have been played there. Now it carries the faster game of croquet. Roses line the hedge behind the terrace, while aubretias and achillea adorn troughs between stone seats. The 'linked hearts' motif, which is featured on the painted ceiling of the castle's Long Gallery, is fashioned in pebbles on the terrace.

Steps lead down to the lawn. The path parallel to the yew alley is edged by a retaining wall, above which are two herbaceous borders. Another such border lies between the path and the lawn.

Below the rose terrace is the oddly named 'Queen's Plot', a mixture of red and pink roses, in a setting that includes verbenas, asters, hebes and potentillas, framed by rock plants along the edge.

The north-facing wall has yews, beneath which are perennials and nasturtiums. Lorimer constructed the corner summerhouse.

The kitchen garden lies to the north end of the topiary garden. Lorimer took the view that there was 'nothing to be ashamed of' in such a garden. Borders of flowers 'backed by low espaliers hanging with shining apples' give it a pleasing character. Espaliers line the grass walk that divides the garden into four, where in each section, respectively, cabbages, potatoes, strawberries and raspberries are grown. Within easy reach of the kitchen door there is also a herb garden. The original two-storey Lorimer tool-shed, built in 1899 and featuring two stone monkeys on the roof-ridge, stands in the north-east corner.

A herring-bone brick pathway leads to the Dowry House, normally used for storing apples. Alongside it, pyrethrums, lilies, irises and paeonies flourish. Another path, lined with Michaelmas daisies and Tree paeonies, leads back to the courtyard.

EDZELL CASTLE

Owner: Historic Scotland

1 mile out of Edzell village off B966

All year during daylight hours

Edzell Castle, built for successive members of the Lindsay family, was at first an L-plan late-15th-century tower house with a barmkin, or defensible courtyard. It was twice extended during the 16th century to meet changing standards of comfort. In 1604, a Pleasance, or formal pleasure garden, was added; in other words, a parterre within a remarkable architectural framework. The chief architect of this civilized splendour was Sir David Lindsay, Lord Edzell, who became a Lord of Session and a member of the Privy Council, but who died in 1610, unfortunately deeply in debt. Mary, Queen of Scots held a meeting of her Privy Council in Edzell; it was visited by James VI; Cromwell's soldiers occupied it in 1651 and shortly before the Jacobite rising, it was purchased by Lord Panmure. For his support of that venture, Panmure's property was forfeited and the castle fell into the hands of the York Building Society, who proceeded to despoil it, the final destruction coming in 1764, when they themselves became bankrupt and the roof and floors were ripped out and sold on behalf of their creditors.

The garden is framed by a wall, finished with heavy coping and semi-circular niches, probably intended to house busts. On the garden side of the wall there are representations of the shamrock, the rose, the thistle and the fleur-de-lys. Inside, the wall is divided all the way round into compartments, once marked off by pilasters the shafts of which are no longer there. On the south side there are thirteen, on the west fourteen. On the east wall there are eight carved panels of the Planetary Deities; on the south wall, representations of the seven Liberal Arts; on the west wall, three Christian Virtues (Faith, Hope and Charity) and four Moral Virtues (Prudence, Temperance, Fortitude and Justice). Between these panels there is, in the words of the official guide (by W Douglas Simpson and Richard Fawcett), 'a gigantic representation of the *fess chequy* of the Lindsays, consisting of three rows of recesses arranged chequer-wise. These recesses are dished, so as to contain flower-boxes, representing heraldic colours.' Above this are the mullets or stars which the Lindsays took over from their predecessors, the Stirlings of Glenesk, carved in relief. The centre of each star has an opening cut into the wall to enable birds to build their nests.

In the other scheme, there is one large oblong recess, also 'dished for flowers' with, above, a sculptured panel. On the east side, these panels are pointed ovals; on the south, arched; on the west, square-headed, each with pierced nesting-places in the wall on both sides of every panel.

At the south-east corner of the Pleasance is a two-storey summerhouse. On the north wall of the upper storey room, all that is left of the castle pannelling may be seen. The bath house—a remarkable adjunct for a 17th-century Scots laird—at the opposite corner of the Pleasance, was pulled down at some stage, but the foundations were excavated in 1855 and have been left exposed.

While the architectural framework is still largely as it originally was in 1604, the actual layout of the garden is necessarily a re-creation, begun in 1934. Those mainly involved were the Inspector of Ancient Monuments for Scotland, James Richardson; W Douglas Simpson, of King's College, Aberdeen, and Sir John Stirling Maxwell, himself an enthusiastic gardener and Chairman of the Ancient Monuments Board for Scotland. Their plan was that terraces should be formed around the edges of the garden with a stepped mound in the middle. At the four corners were to be triangular beds, their designs based on the thistle of Scotland, the rose of England and the fleur-de-lys of France. Within these, and enclosing the central feature, were laid out diagonally-set flower beds with box hedging, shaped to the Lindsay mottoes *dum spiro spero* (while I breathe I hope) and *endure forte* (endure firmly).

Today, their elaborate but charming scheme still prevails. The hedges around the raised terrace walk are of box, those with the mottoes round the diagonal beds, of dwarf box in the shape of thistle, rose and fleur-de-lys. The diagonal beds contain scented floribunda roses of the 'Old Gold' and 'Lili Marlene' varieties. The large yew bush at the centre, surrounded by four smaller bushes, has about it beds of blue and white lobelia, while a red *Tropaeolum speciosum* grows through the central tree. In the chequered recesses of the wall there are now trays of blue and white lobelia, the heraldic colours of the Lindsays, while trays of marigold occupy the larger recesses.

The Pleasance at Edzell is a unique landmark in the history of Scottish gardening and, although compact, is well worth visiting.

Tropaeolum speciosum

FALKLAND PALACE, Falkland, Fife

Owner: The Crown, but in the care of the National Trust for Scotland

Falkland, A912, off A91 from Stirling,
off A92 from Edinburgh

*April to October, Monday to Saturday
from 1000 hours to 1800 hours Sunday 1400 hours to 1800
hours*

Falkland Palace is saturated with Scottish history. James II adopted it as a royal residence. It was enlarged and embellished by James IV and also by James V, who died in it after his defeat at Solway Moss. Mary, Queen of Scots lived in it from time to time; Charles I visited it; Charles II departed from it to face defeat in the field and exile; Cromwell's troops managed to set it on fire. Thereafter, successive Hereditary Keepers allowed it to fall largely into disrepair and in some parts ruin, the Keepership being sold from one family to another.

In 1887, however, that magnificent patron of the arts and of architecture, John Patrick Crichton Stuart, 3rd Marquis of Bute, became Hereditary Keeper by virtue of his descent from the Royal Stuarts. He rebuilt and restored the palace. His grandson, Major Michael Crichton Stuart, made it his home after World War II, and his son, Ninian, the current Hereditary Keeper, still has quarters in the palace. In 1932, the National Trust for Scotland became Deputy Hereditary Keepers.

Falkland was very much the place to which the Stuarts came to relax; by hunting in the hills and hawking; by archery (the main lawn once housed James V's 'long butts' for the practice of archery); and by playing tennis. James V's original tennis court of 1529 was the oldest in these islands, though the surviving court dates from only 1625.

Once, the palace had a large formal garden, though statistical accounts suggest that its chief function was probably the provision of vegetables for the royal kitchen. In one season, it seems, no fewer than eight barrels of onions were delivered by the gardener for the royal table.

The garden was originally surrounded by a wooden

trellis. About 1572, this was replaced by a stone wall, marking the beginning of a number of improvements in the ensuing year under the stewardship of one John Stone. A 'new garden' was apparently laid out in 1628, round about the time the tennis court was reconstructed.

During World War II, the garden was again given over to the production of vegetables. Very soon after hostilities ceased, however, Major Michael Crichton Stuart became Hereditary Keeper, and he engaged Percy Cane to remodel the garden. Cane had recently landscaped the grounds of the Imperial Palace in Addis Ababa.

Though the garden covers only seven acres, Cane accentuated its length and breadth by devising borders around the perimeter and setting out a series of large beds away from the walls. These beds are surrounded by broad grassy walks. The vertical lines of the palace were echoed by these borders.

There are two herbaceous borders. The main one, on the east side, abounds in colour. The smaller border concentrates on pale shades of blue and pink, contrasting with silver and white. Phlox, for instance, characterizes the lower border in the autumn, while the summer season is brought to a colourful rich red end by *Acer griseum* and *Sorbus discolor*.

The lawns contain random specimen trees, including the Cut-leaved beech and the Purple sycamore.

A small north garden features varieties of foliage, and to the west of the garden there is an orchard where cherry and apple trees blossom in early May. The glasshouses, originally by Mackenzie and Moncur of Edinburgh, were rebuilt in 1985, preserving the main features of the originals.

FINLAYSTONE HOUSE

Owner: Mr George MacMillan

Off A8, west of Langbank

All year round from 1000 hours to 1700 hours

Finlaystone was the home of the 15 Earls of Glencairn, the 5th of whom was an ardent supporter of the Reformation. John Knox is said to have held the first Communion of the Reformed Church in the west of Scotland at Finlaystone in 1556. The yew tree under which he did so stood outside the drawing-room window until 1900, when it was moved to its present position because it obscured the light from the sewing of a female member of the Kidston family. The 14th Earl, who was born at Finlaystone, became the friend and patron of Robert Burns, doing much to smooth the poet's introduction to society during his Edinburgh visit in 1786. The house, the heart of which goes back to the 14th century, also has associations with another poet, Alexander Montgomerie, author of *The Cherry and the Slae*.

Finlaystone was added to in 1760 and remodelled by Sir John Burnett for George Kidston, grandfather of the present owner, in 1900, when the garden was laid out in accordance with advice from Messrs Whitton and Goldring of Glasgow and extended to cover about seven and a half acres. Until 1831, when the railway was constructed, the grounds swept down uninterrupted to the River Clyde.

A burn, cascading over several waterfalls, runs through the 'New Garden' to the left of the driveway and by the Old Laundry. The 'New Garden', filled with carefully chosen plants, was created in 1959 by Lady MacMillan, wife of the distinguished soldier, Sir Gordon MacMillan. The burn that runs through it is crossed by an elegant bridge carrying the driveway. On the slopes of the banks of the glen are hostas and azaleas with, further up, weeping cherries.

The main section of the formal garden lies along a gentle north-facing slope overlooking the Clyde and the hills beyond. To the west of the house there is a well-kept private lawn, in which John Knox's tree now flourishes. An unusually trimmed laurel bank runs along the edge facing the river and is fringed by Irish yew and *Pinus radiata*, or Monterey pine. The path reaches to a flight of steps leading to the formal garden, which is surrounded by a pillared yew hedge first castellated by 'an enthusiastic family governess and a French aunt' about 1920. In the centre is a font. A fleur-de-lys mosaic, the petals representing Valour, Wisdom and Faith and repeating a motif found on the cornice of the house, is further west near Lady MacMillan's herbaceous border, created in 1938. This curving area is filled with a lovely selection of perennial plants, providing colour, shape and height.

The lawn on the next highest level is punctuated by shrubbery clumps, which include *Genista hispania*, acers and *Laburnum vossii*; at its eastern end, escallonia, *Berberis stenophylla* and *Hydrangea serrata* flourish. By the path at the top of the lawn, there are splendid plantings of *Rhododendron jacksoni*, *Kalmia latifolia*, *R myrtifolium*, Kurume azaleas, *Hebe cupressoides* and *R davidsonianum*. This garden is rich in interesting shrubs.

To the west of the top lawn there is a charming hexagonal folly, built by the present owner and his staff. The walls came from St Mary's Church, Port Glasgow, demolished in 1984 to make way for road-widening. The rafters came from neighbouring farm buildings, while the floor slates once surrounded a local bowling green. It was thatched in 1987 using Tayside rushes.

Hard by is some Celtic paving laid by Jane MacMillan between 1984 and 1986, to a pattern adapted by Iain Bain from the Book of Kells. Beside it are the remains of a pond, which even modern technology finds difficult to hold intact — the latest polythene lining is regularly punctured by herons! — and a water garden laid out in 1950. In early summer, the entire area is wafted by the scent and enriched by the colours of, among other delights, *Azalea mollis*, *Hamamelis mollis*, *R* 'Bow Bells', *Magnolia stellata*, *Pieris* 'Pink Beauty', *Daphne mezereum*, *Hydrangea acuminata* and *Wiegela variegata*.

At the entrance to the Knot Garden there is a fountain made at Laurencekirk in 1787. This was originally a rose garden. Each bed of the parterre is now surrounded by a dwarf box hedge.

In 1987, Judy Hutton, a daughter of the house, designed the 'Smelly Garden' for the pleasure of blind or handicapped visitors. The walled garden still has its vegetables on the southern side. In the centre is now a brick-pillared circle linked by trellis-work on which roses are being trained. In the centre there will shortly be a fountain. To the north is a fern walk.

There is also a fine stretch of woodland garden on the fringes of which daffodils and bluebells abound in season. Walks guided by a ranger are organized throughout the year.

Maintained largely by the energies of the owning family, the glorious colours of azaleas and rhododendrons in early summer are succeeded by a fine display of roses and, in the autumn, by the spectacular tints of the generous woodland.

Magnolia stellata

FLOORS CASTLE, Kelso

Owner: The Duke of Roxburghe

Entered from Roxburgh Street, Kelso, for Castle, or off B6397 to Walled Garden

Garden Centre in Walled Garden open daily throughout the year

The seat of the Dukes of Roxburghe, Floors (or Fleurs) Castle stands on the outskirts of Kelso not far from the banks of the River Tweed, over which it has commanding views to the Cheviot Hills beyond. It was built in 1718/21 for the 1st Duke of Roxburghe on the site of an earlier house. Both Sir John Vanbrugh and William Adam have been credited with its architecture. Adam was certainly supervising operations there in 1723 and, indeed, claimed credit for it in his *Vitruvius Scoticus*. In 1849/50, however, the Castle was so extensively remodelled in the Caroline style by Sir William H Playfair for the 6th Duke that neither Vanbrugh nor Adam would have recognised it! It was said after the completion of this transformation to be 'one of the most palatial residences of the Scottish nobility' and was visited by Queen Victoria and various members of her family. Playfair was also responsible for the Home Farm buildings to the rear of the Castle and for the extension of the 'already beautiful garden' between 1857/60.

The Walled Garden, an exceptionally large one, lies some distance from the Castle, but a bus plies between the two. Behind the first long herbaceous border, espaliered pears and apples form a fence. The plants here and on the opposite side flower earlier in the season but when they are past, the other borders take over. There are lupins, penstemons in variety, hollyhocks, aquilegias and delphiniums. At right angles, in the double herbaceous border, later colour is supplied by large clumps of annuals, huge masses of purple Michaelmas daisies, golden rod and phlox. Again at right angles, there are two more borders backed on either side by pillared roses which are trained to form a solid barrier. The areas at the end, two of several, are filled with every hue of dahlia. Indeed, anyone considering increasing a dahlia collection would be well advised to visit this garden. Each block of flowers is meticulously named and the colour spectrum is remarkable. Apart from the reds, yellows and oranges, there are the subtle shades of the peach/pinks like 'Dawn Sky', 'Raffles' and 'Raiser's Ideal'. There are, literally, hundreds of dahlias of every form.

Traditionally, Scottish Walled Gardens include vegetables as well as fruit and flowers and at Floors there are beds of asparagus and the huge Kelsae onions for which, as the name suggests, the Borders are famous. Fruit trees are trained up the sheltering high walls and in the impeccably kept greenhouses there are carnations and begonias.

To some, the huge masses of colour might seem rather overpowering, containing little that is rare or unusual, but the overall impression is one of rainbow splendour. For those exhausted by such a palette of colour, there is an admirable little tea-room with homebaking.

Dahlia 'COMET'

GEILSTON HOUSE, Cardross

Owner: National Trust for Scotland: (presently occupied by Miss Bell)

Off A814 Dumbarton to Helensburgh road almost immediately on the right past Cardross village

The garden is open only on specified days for which the **Gardens of Scotland** *handbook should be consulted*

Built, according to the official listing, for the Geils family, Geilston House, with its crow-stepped gables, dates from the 18th century and has a contemporary doocot. There are some who maintain that the oldest part of the L-shaped house dates from the 15th century. Be that as it may, it has been much added to. A keystone in the old potting shed carries the date 1797, which may well be the date when the stone-walled garden was constructed.

The two ladies, whose combined skill created the present beautifully varied garden out of the traditional Victorian one which preceded it, were Miss Bell, the daughter of Sir Thomas Bell, a one-time Managing Director of the ship-builder John Brown of Clydebank, and her friend Miss Hendry, whose father, a Glasgow ship chandler, bought the house from the Geils family in 1925. Miss Bell alone survives. House and garden have been made over to the National Trust for Scotland, though the garden will not be open to the general public during Miss Bell's lifetime. With its varied beauties, it seems certain, in due course, to become one of the Trust's gems in the Central Scotland area.

A long drive, fairly recently planted with limes, leads up to the house. On the left beyond the potting sheds is the vegetable garden, largely now given over to grass, but which is still divided by immaculately trimmed privet and beech hedges. Here there are strawberry, raspberry and gooseberry beds, along with dahlias and chrysanthemums. Outside the rear precincts of the house, Morello cherries flourish on the wall. This is the woodland area through which a stream winds down to a waterfall, which in turn is fed from the lily-pond by another waterfall, once used to drive the old Cardross sawmill.

The woodland area contains a great many mature conifers and broadwoods, together with rhododendrons, including not a few from world-famous Bodnant. Geilston is noted for its acers, such as the weeping *Acer palmatum* 'Dissectum atropurpureum', *Acer griseum* with its fascinating peeling bark and the very rare *Acer shindschejojo* in the Walled Garden. Another tree whose bark peels is the *Prunus serula* from Western China, here in fine fettle. There is also a magnificent *Acer platanoides* 'Crimson King' which adds to this garden's glorious autumn colouring.

Fierce winds from the south-west assail the northern coast of the River Clyde, as can be seen from the thinning sides of some of the trees; but within the sheltered Walled Garden, the borders are filled with every kind of interesting shrub. There are far too many to be listed, but among the more special ones, you will find an unusual *Pittosporum tenuifolium atropurpureum*, *Acer negundo* 'Flamingo', a variegated *Stranvæsia*, *Philadelphus aureus*, a standard 'Canary Bird' rose, espaliered apples and a huge *Sequoiadendron giganteum* which dominates the lawn. At the top of the garden a royal fern, *Osmunda regalis*, rises up amongst neighbouring azaleas.

A focal point near the house is a delightful little birdbath whose cherub seems to be gazing appreciatively at the heaths (about 90 varieties) and roses around and beneath him and towards a magnificent *Hydrangea paniculata* 'Grandiflora'.

On the walls, there is a lovely *Ceanothus* 'Gloire de Versailles' and below it a long border of miniature azaleas.

In the slope to the side, there is a *Eucryphia nymansensis* and a *Cercidiphyllum japonicum* from China and Japan, absolutely breath-catching in its autumn colouring, as well as the uncommon *Disanthus cercidifolius* and *Ceratostigma*, equally lovely at the same time of year. Below in the glen, once the scratching area for chickens, a further garden is being laid out.

Another double herbaceous border contains a magnolia which flowers twice in the year, a *Sorbus cashmiriana* and also a pale yellow-berried 'Joseph Rock' as well as a host of colourful perennials.

Up the nearside path from the burn, there are more plants to delight—a *Euonymous europaeus* with intriguing scarlet seedpods and another, *E alatus*, which grows in tiers. There are viburnums and a fascinating little purple spotted *Tricyrtis*, or toad lily.

Donald Calder has been in charge of Geilston for 13 years and works happily all the hours of daylight to keep his domain in perfect order. This wonderful garden is a tribute to the horticultural skills of the two remarkable ladies who created it and, incidentally, who were also in their day first-class golfers.

Osmunda regalis

GLASGOW BOTANIC GARDEN

Owner: Glasgow District Council

Great Western Road, at junction of Byres Road and Queen Margaret Drive

Daily from 1000 hours to 1645 hours, 1615 hours in winter

Work on the first Glasgow Botanic Garden was begun on 15 May 1817, on an eight-acre site at Sandyford, at the west end of Sauchiehall Street. Previously there had been a Physic garden, established in 1705 in the grounds of the Old College and maintained for teaching purposes for more than a century. The initiative for the establishment of the Sandyford garden came from Thomas Hopkirk of Dalbeth, an estate at the east end of Glasgow, who founded the Royal Botanic Garden Institution of Glasgow to run it. Funds to finance this garden were raised by public subscription. The University made a substantial contribution on the understanding that plant material for students should be supplied in perpetuity, and that a room was set aside in which the Professor of Botany could deliver lectures.

When the move to Sandyford was made, many of the plants for the new Botanic Garden came from Hopkirk's own garden at Dalbeth. Sir Ilay Campbell of Succoth became the first president, with Hopkirk as vice-president and Stewart Murray the first curator. The first Regius Professor of Botany, Dr Robert Graham, was appointed in the same year, although the work of laying out the new Gardens was largely left to Murray and Hopkirk, whose *Flora Glottiana*, published in 1813, a documented list of the wild plants of the Clyde district, was one of the first of its kind to be published in the United Kingdom.

One of the most distinguished botanists of all time, Sir William Hooker was appointed to the Chair of Botany in 1821. During the next ten years he raised the Glasgow Botanic Garden to a position of considerable eminence in botanical circles. Two years after the move in 1839 to the present West End site, Sir William left Glasgow to become the first Director of the Royal Botanic Gardens at Kew, when it became a public institution.

The range of glasshouses was moved to the new site, along with many of the plants, although the only known survivor is the weeping ash growing to the south of the main lawn. The new gardens were first opened to members of the Institution on 30 April 1842. The annual family subscription was one guinea (105 pence). The public was admitted on Saturdays for one shilling (5 pence), and on certain days, for one old penny each, the Gardens were 'thrown open to the Working Classes'.

Today, the most interesting features of the Gardens are generally held to be the glasshouses, the most striking of which is the curvilinear Kibble Palace, occupying 23 000 square feet and one of the largest in Britain. Apart from its collection of plants, it exhibits a series of elegant Victorian marble statues by Hamo Thornycroft, Goscombe John and others. It had originally been built in 1860 on the Coulport, Loch Long, estate of an enterprising (if eccentric) engineer, John Kibble. In 1873 he sold it to Glasgow. It was dismantled, shipped up the River Clyde and re-erected and extended in the Botanic Gardens. He intended to run it as a concert hall, a use for which it soon proved unsuitable, although both Gladstone and Disraeli delivered rectorial addresses from its pond, covered in for the occasion. Kibble soon lost interest in managing it and in 1881 the Institution, on the strength of a loan from the Corporation, bought out the lease and converted the Kibble Palace into a winter garden. By 1885, Glasgow Corporation as creditors had entered into possession of an asset that still lay outwith the city boundaries, paying £59 531 for it. In 1891, when the City of Glasgow Act was passed, the Botanic Gardens were transferred from the ownership of the Institution to the Corporation. Soon after, the fine collection of Tree ferns and plants from temperate areas of the world was established under the great glass dome, with many forms of *Camellia japonica* round the outer ring.

The corridor houses plants from the southern area of Africa, including the Silver tree, *Leucodendron argenteum*; Arum lily, *Zantedeschia aethiopica*; *Sparmannia africana* and Cape heaths, or Bell heathers. Although heaths are common in Britain, there are many more species in South Africa.

In the south-west corner are examples of Australian flora, including Kangaroo Paw, *Anigozanthus spp* and *Kennedya rubicunda*. Acacias include *A dealbata* and the Sydney Golden wattle, *A longifolia*. There are also plants from New Zealand, South and North America, China, Japan and the Mediterranean region. There are two exhibition wings. In the north wing, the development of 'The Plant Kingdom' from the Cambrian Period (570 million years ago), through a collection of fossils, to the Quaternary Period (2½ million years ago) is traced.

The main range of glasshouses near the summit of the hill (the other side of which slopes down to the River Kelvin), includes a conservatory for a colourful display of flowers throughout the year, as well as glasshouses for orchids, begonias, temperate economic plants, succulents, a Palm House, tropical economic plants, tropical ferns, stove plants, tropical flowers and an Aquatic House.

In the 20s and 30s of the present century, the Botanic Garden was the favourite place for nannies to perambulate with their youthful charges, sitting on the long row of seats along the main avenue to exchange below-stairs gossip. At the highest point of the park there once stood a Victorian bandstand, much used until World War II.

Today, the white-starched nannies have gone. Many of those who still crowd into the Gardens to walk or sit in the sun probably have no great interest in the well-labelled plant layouts. But there is a herb garden; a rock garden containing many alpine plants; summer bedding displays on the slopes in front of the glasshouses; a large double herbaceous border; a systematic garden and a chronological border, set out to show when some of the more common garden plants were first introduced to these islands. It is laid out in beds, one for each century from the 16th to the 20th.

Over the hill, on the banks of the Kelvin, is the Arboretum, created in 1975 out of a former rubbish dump, and best approached from the Kirklee Gate and Ford Road end. A collection of plants introduced by David Douglas is being built up here, together with a collection of tertiary relics—trees and shrubs that are known from fossil remains and, except in a few restricted areas, killed off during the Ice Age. These include the gingko (found as a fossil on the island of Mull); the metasequoia, the magnolia and cercidiphyllum.

GLENARN, Rhu

Owners: Michael and Sue Thornley and family

A814, ¼ mile beyond Rhu, off Pier Road

Daily from 21 March to 21 June
from dawn to dusk

In 1837 Professor McGeorge, a friend of Sir William Hooker (the first holder of the Chair of Botany at Glasgow University), built the house at Glenarn beside a wooded glen above what was then the small village of Rhu, overlooking the Gareloch. It was McGeorge who laid out the original structure of the garden. In 1849–50 Joseph Hooker (the younger) visted Sikkim, sending back seeds to the owners of several west-coast gardens, Glenarn among them. The glens and winding paths that exist today were laid out in the 1880s.

In 1927, Archie and Sandy Gibson acquired Glenarn. Guided by the eccentric stockbroker John Holmes (who began but, for financial reasons, failed to complete several houses, including Robert Lorimer's Formakin in Renfrewshire), the Gibsons cleared the ground to make room for new plants, particularly rhododendrons, then being much imported by overseas plant collectors. Throughout the 30s the collection expanded, taking in among other specimens *R baileyi, R lindleyi* (both bred from Ludlow and Sherriff seed) and *R luteiflorum,* and *R zeylanicum* by Frank Kingdon Ward. During the later 30s, magnolias, daffodils, naturalized Candelabra primulas and various forms of meconopsis were introduced to the woodland setting. After World War II, the success of the Gibsons' early efforts in hybridizing unusually large-leaved crosses became increasingly evident. Up the left hand path from the entrance may also be seen *R falconeri,* grown from the 1849 Hooker seed and still surviving, as is *R thomsonii,* as well as a large *R macabeanum* and a fine *R* 'John Holms'. Further up to the right of 'The Burn', *R sinogrande,* its leaves the largest of the species, continues to flourish.

Beside the house there is a daffodil lawn, a charming rock garden and at its base, beside the lawn, a dramatically lovely blood-red *R arboreum.* Across the 'Sunnyside Path' lies a quarry garden containing dwarf rhododendrons and Candelabra primulas in a range of colours and meconopses. At the top of the path there is a fine *R* 'Ronald'.

Lower down this slope, there are magnolias, a splendid Wellingtonia, *Sequoiadendron giganteum*, another *R lindleyi* and *R maddenii* with its lily-like flowers. Glenarn also contains other acid-loving plants such as camellias, crinodendrons and embothriums.

In 1975, Archie Gibson and his wife both died. Sandy survived until 1978. The Thornleys bought the property in 1983 and are still in the process of lovingly restoring what has always been regarded as one of the best rhododendron gardens in the west of Scotland.

Rhododendron falconeri

GLENWHAN GARDEN, Dunragit

Owners: Mr and Mrs Knott

7 miles east of Stranraer, 1 mile up the Glenwhan road off the A75 at Dunragit

April to September daily from noon to 1700 hours (closed Mondays, except Bank Holidays)

There is a popular belief that great gardens must necessarily be old gardens. The achievement of the Knotts at Glenwhan disposes of this notion, for in 14 years they have restored and added a wing to a formerly dilapidated house and cultivated round it, with the addition of two small and picturesque lochans (created by damming the marshland), a garden of quite remarkable loveliness. Paths lead the visitor round the lochans and up a wooded hill to a gazebo, from which on a good day the Isle of Man may be seen, and back round the house, affording magnificent views over Luce Bay and the Mull of Galloway.

When the garden was started, the marshy hillside was covered in bracken and gorse. Now, among the winding paths may be seen rhododendrons, azaleas, shrubs in variety including hydrangeas, *Olearia haastii,* cistus and osmanthus. Here, too, are shrub roses and a healthy specimen of the unusual perennial, *Podophyllum emodi.* The rocky outcrops provide a natural habitat for alpines and heaths, while the lochans are home to damp-loving genera, such as water-lilies and bull-rushes. Here you will find magnificent clumps of deep-red crocosmia in late summer, and in the spring, a host of bluebells, snowdrops and daffodils flourishing under sorbus and willow. Each year, yet another part of the land is being taken into cultivation to enhance what has already been a remarkable achievement. For instance, a woodland walk is in the process of being planted.

Mr and Mrs Knott do their own propagating and have established a nursery from which plants may be purchased. There is also a welcome little tearoom.

This garden covering comparatively few acres (in relation to some others which have been described), will be an inspiration to many and should not be missed by anyone visiting the area. Although a recently created garden, it gives the impression of having been lovingly established over many years.

At Glenwhan, we came upon a locally adapted verse by the late Lady Macconachie, the original of which first appeared in the *The Scotsman* newspaper in 1963, and which, with their permission, we reprint here:

> A Dire Warning!
> Awake my muse, bring bell and book
> to curse the hand that cuttings took.
> May every kind of garden pest,
> his little plot of ground infest,
> who stole the plants at Inverewe,
> from Falkland Palace, Glenwhan too.
> Let caterpillars, capsid bugs,
> leafhoppers, thrips, all sorts of slugs,
> play havoc with his garden plot,
> and a late frost destroy the lot.

Crocosmia x crocosmiiflora

GREENBANK GARDENS AND ADVICE CENTRE

Owner: The National Trust for Scotland

From Clarkston Toll, Mearns Road to Flenders Road,
½ mile to the right. From Eastwood Toll, off
Kilmarnock Road A77, 1 mile to the left

*All year round (except 25–6 December
and 1–2 January) from 0930 hours to sunset*

Greenbank was built in 1764 on the site of Flenders Farm
for Robert Allason, a major supplier to ships, who ran
into financial difficulties as a result of the American War
of Independence. Consequently, in 1784 he sold the
estate to one of his creditors, Thomas Pate. Five years
later he sold it to Alan Lightbody; but in 1794, Lightbody
also got into financial difficulties and had to sell
Greenbank to pay his debts. After a period of ownership
by the Hutcheson family, it was acquired by John
Hamilton of Rogerton, East Kilbride. His family owned it
through four generations. On the death of the last
Hamilton, Greenbank passed to a nephew, Sheriff
Young, who in 1962 sold it to Mr W P Blyth. He
sympathetically restored the garden; then in 1976
offered it to the National Trust for Scotland. Recently,
the house, too, has come into the possession of the
Trust and is now their headquarters in the West of
Scotland.

The garden, covering two and a half acres, is entered
from the side. It consists of two broad paths running
lengthways and sideways, bisected in the middle by a
hedged circle containing a lectern sundial dating from
about 1620, and hence older than the house. A series of
gardens is separated mostly by further hedges. The
borders along the path to the sundial contain shrubs,
including roses, and herbaceous perennials. From the
sundial, looking towards the house, a tall Wellingtonia,
Sequoiadendron giganteum, can be seen rising behind
it. The semi-circular beds surrounding the sundial are
used for a colourful display of bulbs in spring and
bedding plants in summer.

Walking away from the house, on the left is the raised
bed garden, once a tennis court. It has a pool with
running water and was designed for the enjoyment of

disabled visitors. A collection of ferns is situated near the potting shed and the walls support several varieties of clematis. The glasshouse and the potting shed, not normally open to the public, were designed to enable disabled people to work in them. The borders of the main walk have mixed trees and shrubs, including old fruit trees (through which roses mingle), retained for their aesthetic rather than their fruit-bearing qualities.

On the left of the main path, moving back towards the house, are the Echium and Spring Gardens, the latter given over to heathers, conifers and bulbs. *Erica carnea* and *Calluna vulgaris* flourish here. The conifers include *Picea glauca* 'Albertiana' and a *Pinus artistata,* an example of what is believed to be the world's oldest growing plant.

The path borders contain a wide selection of colourful shrubs and plants. On the far wall to the left there is a small rock garden, with, beyond the lateral hedge, a grassy lawn containing a pool to accommodate Pilkington Jackson's statue, cast for the Glasgow Empire Exhibition of 1938, and now played on by fountains.

HILL OF TARVIT

Owner: The National Trust for Scotland

Off the A916, 2½ miles south of Cupar, Fife

*Gardens all year round from 1000 hours to sunset;
house from 3 April to 31 October at seasonally specified
times*

In one sense Hill of Tarvit is a monument to an act of
vandalism, for when, in 1904, the Dundee jute tycoon
Frederick Bower Sharp acquired Sir William Bruce's
Wemyss Hall, built in 1696, it was almost totally
destroyed to make way for the present house. It was
completed by Robert Lorimer in 1906 and designed as a
showcase for the owner's rich collection of Flemish
tapestries, Chinese porcelain and bronze, European
paintings and other art treasures.

Lorimer designed the gardens on the south side of the
house: Sharp, a keen horticulturalist who employed
seven gardeners, those to the north. Both men were
agreed that the house should be surrounded by green,
with no colour near the frontage. To the south there is
therefore a series of terraced lawns, encircled by
trimmed yew hedges and linked by elegant stairs. Trees
in the surrounding woodlands planted at this time
include *Eucryphia glutinosa*, which foams white in
August; a *Parrotia*; a *Garrya* and some exceptionally fine
rhododendrons in which Sharp was particularly
interested.

The sunken rose gardens at either side of the house
(invisible from the house itself) were part of the original
Lorimer design, although Sharp made various not
unsympathetic alterations to Lorimer's plan.

The herbaceous border is a more recent creation. The
original walled garden, now let out to a commercial
concern, contains a range of Victorian glasshouses with
a central conservatory.

Sharp was also a financier, indeed, chairman of one of
Scotland's first investment trusts. His son Hugh, born in
1897, served as an artillery officer in World War I; then
went to Oxford before becoming involved in the family
financial concerns. He, too, was a keen horticulturalist,

and brought back some unusual plants from his foreign travels. His fine collection of botanical books is now housed at the Trust's gardening school at Threave.

Frederick Sharp died, aged 70, in 1932. Hugh, on his way to meet his fiancée by train rather than by road because of snowy conditions, was killed in the Castlecary rail disaster of 1937.

Frederick's widow died in 1946. Two years later, the 38-year-old unmarried daughter, Elizabeth, died of cancer. She bequeathed the estate and the house and its contents to the National Trust for Scotland, though for 30 years thereafter, by her wish, the top flat was used as a convalescent home by the Marie Curie Foundation. In 1977, following the building of a hospice in Dundee, the Trust came into full possession.

As is often the case where landscape is concerned, perhaps it is rather more the views from the garden at Hill of Tarvit than the garden itself that are of most interest; but, of course, the layout of a Lorimer garden, even a minor one, is always of considerable interest to many visitors. There is a particularly fine view of the Fife hills from the slopes behind the house. Through the magnificent wrought-iron gates, by Thomas Hadden of Edinburgh, there are pleasing woodland walks.

Garrya elliptica

INVERARAY CASTLE, Argyll

Owner: The Duke of Argyll

On A83 Arrochar to Lochgilphead road, just short of the town

Policies including the woodland walk open throughout the year; garden by written prior arrangement

The history of Inveraray is essentially that of the Earls and Dukes of Argyll — Campbells, one of the most powerful of the Scottish clans. Their ancestor was Sir Colin Campbell of Lochow, knighted in 1280. In 1445, Sir Colin Campbell was raised to the Scottish peerage as Lord Campbell. Archibald, the 8th Earl, was created Marquis in 1641 and ten years later crowned Charles II at Scone. The 10th Earl was created Duke of Argyll in 1701. The United Kingdom Dukedom was created in 1892.

The Marquis who crowned Charles II appears in Scott's novel *The Legend of Montrose*, in which the Argyll residence was then the much-admired 'noble old Gothic castle of Inveraray, whose varied outline, embattled walls, towers and outer and inner courts' were replaced by the 3rd Duke. He commissioned one R Morris to build the present rather undistinguished edifice between 1744 and 1761. (The remains of the original castle can still be seen from the carpark.) It was greatly damaged by fire in 1877 and again almost a century later, though in both cases effectively restored.

The policies, overlooking Loch Fyne, were planned by the 8th and 9th Earls in the 17th century, with advice from the well-known silviculturalist John Evelyn. The gardens had been begun in 1744 by the 3rd Duke. They were re-landscaped in 1848 for the 8th Duke, who employed W A Nesfield. His other work at the time included the Rose Garden at the Royal Botanic Garden at Kew. Morris had a further hand in the reshaping of the landscaping when the present castle was built. The formal Rose Garden was extensively replanted by the 11th Duke during the 1950s.

Johnson and Boswell visited Inveraray on 25 October 1773, when Johnson so charmed one of the other guests, Lady Betty Hamilton, that after dinner, 'she placed her chair close to his and leaned upon the back of it', listening eagerly to what the great man had to say.

Inveraray enjoys, or endures, a high rainfall, vigorous winter winds but comparatively little frost. Nevertheless the plant life continues to flourish.

The border to the side of the castle is planted with ericas and guarded by a small statue of Richard the Lion Heart. On the other side of the path there are azaleas, some of them of recent planting, *Hydrangea paniculata*, acers and at the bottom a magnificent *Magnolia acuminata* (the oddly named Cucumber Tree, so-called because of its small gherkin-like fruits).

Nearby, there is an ancient millstone (normally housing a statue of Nancy Cunard, but which was out on loan when we visited) in the centre of which, it is alleged, a rowan tree once grew. Many superstitions pertain in Scotland to this tree which was supposed to keep away witches. The gentleman who broke the tree when trying to remove the heavy stone died of a heart attack, though probably because of exertion rather than from any potent spell cast by a malevolent hag!

The Rose Garden contains hundreds of roses, many of them scented. A solution of Epsom salts, we were told, enhances their perfume.

Opposite this area, much of the ground is in the process of being cleared, or heavily cut down. While still somewhat overgrown, the bright scarlet seeds of *Paeony mlokosewitchii* are particularly striking in autumn.

The chief interest of the garden, however, lies in the ancient trees. There is a very remarkable aged *Thuja plicata* which has now assumed the shape of a central tree (the mother) with a circle of trees forming her offspring, and very sturdy children they are too. There is an equally ancient *Sequoiadendron giganteum* (and it is gigantic); a chestnut which has a recorded history of over 400 years and a *Taxus baccata* so old that its boughs have formed several arcs from one side of the glade to the other. The avenue to the rear of the castle is lined with magnificent ancient limes.

The walls of the fosse round the base of the castle are clothed with a variety of shrubs and the windows look out on immaculately cut lawns.

In spring, the extensive grassy areas, sloping down to the roadside and the 18th century hump-backed bridge leading into the town, are aglow with daffodils.

Mr Bowe, the present gardener, is pleased to show visitors around the garden, provided a prior appointment has been made by letter.

Paeonia mlokosewitschii

INVERESK LODGE

Owner: The National Trust for Scotland

A1 Edinburgh to Dunbar road, and then A614 to Inveresk

*All year round Monday–Friday 1000 hours to 1630 hours
Sunday 1400 hours to 1700 hours from Easter to 30
September
Saturday 1400 hours to 1700 hours in summer only*

The still relatively unspoiled village of Inveresk—the name in Gaelic means 'the confluence of the waters'—stands above the right bank of the River Esk. The village has its place in Scottish literature because the Reverend Alexander ('Jupiter') Carlyle ministered there for 57 years. He was largely responsible for breaking the anti-theatre attitude of the Church of Scotland, and for a singularly racy *Autobiography*. Seventeenth-century Inveresk Lodge, the oldest surviving house in the village, was gifted to the National Trust for Scotland in 1959 by Mrs Helen E Brunton.

There is documented evidence of a garden at Inveresk from 1881. The plan was, in fact, found by happy coincidence after the present lay-out was completed. The new garden, designed and completed by Eric Robson, then the Trust's Garden Adviser, turned out to have been based broadly on the 1881 plan. It was then intended to be a demonstration garden, like Greenbank, Glasgow, or Suntrap at Gogar, near Edinburgh. Since 1985, however, work has been going on carrying through a programme of renewal, one bed a year, based on the Royal Horticultural Society's list of plants (of which there are some 3 500 to choose from).

The house, owned by the National Trust, is rented out and is not open to the public.

As one would expect in any National Trust for Scotland garden, Inveresk is in immaculate condition, with almost every plant being meticulously named. The long herbaceous border at the entrance contains all kinds of treasures from the six-foot-high Tree paeonies to the delightful tiny flowers of *Aster ericoides* 'Silver Spray'. Twiggy *Corylopsis pauciflora* contrasts with the spiky heads of eryngium, as does the bushy *Carpentaria californica* with the strap-like leaves of Day lilies, hemerocallis.

Because of the sheltering high wall behind, many tender things survive at Inveresk where they would not elsewhere in other gardens. The same high wall carries a splendid range of climbing roses including such old favourites as 'Albertine', 'Veilchenblau', 'Emily Gray', 'Fantin-Latour' and 'New Dawn'.

The various sections of lawn are punctuated by several beds each containing unusual specimens. For instance, there is a fine example of the *Matteuccia struthiopteris* fern, a *Tiarella cordifolia* (foam flower), *Sisyrinchium striatum* and the lovely *Geranium wallichianum* 'Buxton's Blue', amongst others.

At the end of one lawn, a huge stone container has been carefully placed under the delicate leaves of *Pyrus salcifolia pendula*. An air of formality has been added to an otherwise most carefully controlled informality, with the introduction of four conical junipers. A further border contains the lovely pink *Crinum powellii*, so useful for providing colour in late summer.

The long greenhouses contain a range of interesting plants such as *Cestrum elegans* with its rosy-red racemes, *Prostanthera rotundifolia*, plumbago, *Jasminum mesnyi*, camellias and vines.

This is a delightful garden, particularly for those who wish to plan future variety in their plant stock and who may also wish to discover how plants can be set out to their best advantage.

INVEREWE GARDENS

Owner: The National Trust for Scotland

On A832, by Poolewe, 6 miles north-east of Gairloch

*All year from 0900 hours to 2100 hours
(dusk if earlier)*

During the 1860s, the widow of the Laird of Gairloch, in Wester Ross, Lady Mary Mackenzie, bought the lands of Kernsary and Inverewe for her son, Osgood, then about 22. Osgood's half-brother Francis, the sixth baronet and thirteenth Laird of Gairloch, had inherited both the family title and estates (acquired, incidentally, by force from the Macleods in the 15th century), thus leaving Osgood free to pursue his passionate interest in gardens. His land included the peninsula Am Ploc Ard, 'the high lump', at Inverewe, 90 mountainy miles from Inverness, the nearest town of any size. At that time it was a windswept wilderness of stunted heather and crowberry and, according to his daughter, Mrs Mairi Sawyer, 'one small willow tree' which 'stood all by itself on a heather moorland in the Highlands of Scotland'. It has often been remarked that the truly astonishing thing about Inverewe is not so much the extraordinary beauty, variety and scenic quality of the garden as the fact that a garden exists at all in such an unrewarding location, albeit on a shoreline washed by the beneficent Gulf Stream.

Mackenzie began by planting trees as shelter for his 60 or so exposed acres. Being a man of infinite patience, he waited about 15 years for them to grow tall enough to provide shelter for the tender plants for which he intended to provide a loving home. At the same time, he built for himself a turreted Scots Baronial-style mansion, unfortunately destroyed by fire in 1914. Stones from the original house were used to construct the rock garden. The modern house, designed in the style of Dutch South African homesteads, (not open to the public) was built in 1937 for Mrs Sawyer, who carried on her father's work in the garden after his death in 1922.

A word should be said about this remarkable lady, because she became one of Scotland's outstanding women gardeners. By the time she was a young

124

teenager, her parents' marriage had broken up. She elected to go with her father. For 60 of the 90 years when the garden was under Mackenzie control, she was involved with it, first in partnership with her father and then on her own. She was married first to her cousin, Ronald Hanbury—both their children died in infancy giving rise to the legend of a curse put upon the family for dislodging the crofters who formerly lived on the site of the garden—and after being widowed in 1933, she married Ronald Sawyer. Both men shared her gardening passion.

A year before her own death in 1953, anxious that the garden she and her father had so painstakingly created should always be available for all who wished to see it, she donated it with an endowment to the National Trust for Scotland. In 1952, the garden had about 3 000 visitors per annum; today it has over 120 000.

The National Trust for Scotland's guidebook divides the garden into 19 sections to make the visitor's experience easier to organize, and is a model of its kind. The record of the creation of the garden is contained in Osgood Mackenzie's own book, *A Hundred Years in the Highlands*, a Scottish gardening classic first published in 1922, just before he died, and reissued in our own time. We shall follow roughly the Trust's route here, since it is the one most likely to be followed by visitors, depending on their stamina or the time at their disposal.

On the gate lodge wall there is a lovely *Crinodendron hookerianum* with its red lantern-like flowers and, among other plants, fine examples of *Senecio elaeagnifolius*, *Griselinia littoralis* 'Variegata', olearia, *Kniphofia caulescens* and *meconopsis x sheldonii*.

The drive, which runs from the gate lodge to the house, contains, amongst other early Mackenzie plantings, a superb *Eucalyptus coccifera* from Tasmania and, from New Zealand, an *Olearia moschata*. To provide seasonal colour, there are azaleas, camellias, shrub roses and such perennials as irises, bergenias, hostas and lilies as well as the vivid orange *Euphorbia griffithii*. The wide variety of rhododendrons includes an ancient, if slightly askew, *R falconeri*, *R dryophyllum*, *R ciliatum*,

R barbatum and *R thomsonii*, amongst others. Romping through the rather vulgar *R ponticum*, there is a vivid red Chilean Flame Flower, *Tropaeolum speciosum*, so much at home in our northern climate.

Turning left off the drive, the visitor comes to the first of Inverewe's herbaceous borders, at their best during July and August. Mrs Sawyer was very critical of these and set them out only against her better judgement and because of vigorous persuasion.

Across the path is the rock garden, on the higher shelf of which celmisias, *longifolium* and *munroi*, and raoulias, both *glabra* and *hookeri*, thrive. Also to be seen here are *Anemone alpina* 'Sulphurea'; the gentians, *acaulis* and *verna*; *Daphne arbuscula* and *Helichrysum coralloides*. The lower level contains *Anemone leveillei*; *Euryops acraeus*, and the rhododendrons *aperantum* and *impeditum*, among other interesting plants.

From this area, too, may be seen to advantage another *Eucalyptus coccifera* and a *Cordyline indivisa*, and beyond the house a noble sequoiadendron from California; a European Silver fir, *Abies alba*, now over 100 feet in height, and a Douglas fir, grown from seed planted over 130 years ago.

The Japanese section was named after a now vanished Japanese cherry. Dry soil, shade and protection from frost give shelter to such plants as the Tree fern, *Dicksonia antartica* and *Trachycarpus fortunei*, as well as the lovely sweet-smelling Mexican Orange Blossom, *Choisya ternata*. euphorbia, hosta and *Veratrum album* also find these conditions to their liking.

The woodland section of Inverewe contains the original shelter trees, mainly Scots and Corsican pine, as well as beech, sycamore and rhododendron *Ponticum* (now proving a menace over much of the Highlands, but much favoured here by Mackenzie), and the New Zealand shrub *Griselinia littoralis*, planted by Mrs Sawyer. Fierce gales in 1953, 1983 and 1984 (in which year the wind force reached 120 miles per hour) uprooted 192 trees and finally blew away the wind-recording machine itself. A *Rhododendron giganteum*, grown from seed sent from China by the plant collector George Forrest, is passed on the way to the small pond, which features primulas of many rare varieties, as well as meconopsis in May and June, together with *Iris chrysographes* and *I forrestii*. There are several varieties of rhododendrons growing on the peat bank including *R campanulatum* 'Aeruginosum', *R stewartianum* and *R fastuosum* 'Flore-Pleno'.

The Wet Valley is dominated by the huge-leaved *Gunnera manicata,* and a splendid specimen this one is. Among the plants here is the native *Ourisia* 'Loch Ewe', a cross between *O coccinea* and *O macrophylla* made by a former head gardener, Geoffrey Collins.

The larger pond garden features *Hosta* 'Frances Williams' and several examples of *Nymphaea*, notably *alba*, 'James Brydon', *marliacea* 'Chromatella', and 'Sunrise'.

The rhododendron walk contains some of Mackenzie's first plantings, including the two large-leaved *R sinogrande* and *R hodgsonii*. Notable also is the New Zealand Tree fern, *Dicksonia squarrosa* and the Umbrella plant *Peltiphyllum peltatum* which flowers in February, then opens umbrella-like leaves that, uniquely at Inverewe, turn red and orange in autumn.

The Peace Plot of 1919 commemorates the end of World War I and has various species of meconopsis and primula and a fine rhododendron, *zeylanicum*.

One of the first areas Mackenzie established is that known as Bambooselem, where many of the original plants survive, including several large trees such as *Eucalyptus cordata* and a larch covered in the climbing *Hydrangea petiolaris*. *Davidia involucrata* is here, with its large white, handkerchief-like flowers in May, as well as the March-flowering, magnificent *magnolia camp-bellii*. In spring, the path leading from this area is carpeted with an American Dog's Tooth violet, *Erythronium revolutum*.

The American area and its environs feature many handsome trees and plants. Here you will find *Orchis elata, Cordyline indivisa* and *Lobelia tupa* from Chile, as well as a further range of rhododendrons.

The final area to be inspected is the walled garden. The constructing of the wall for it, and the subsequent transportation of the soil in creels, are described in detail in Mackenzie's book. Here there is established the second herbaceous border, at its best in June and early July. On the walls behind, a *Clematis rehderiana* from Chile clambers up. Opposite this border is a collection of shrub and species roses.

Along the bottom of the garden runs a narrow plot of annuals that flower in mid summer.

The Victorian range of glasshouses contains period conservatory plants and, in another section, orchids and bromeliads. The modern glasshouse was built to honour Mackenzie's kinsman, David Ogilvy, with funds provided by the Scottish National Golden Jubilee Fund (USA).

It is manifestly impossible to do full justice in this brief context to the enormous variety of rare plants and trees Inverewe contains. If, however, a visitor to Scotland, for whatever unlikely reason, found himself able to visit only one garden, then undoubtedly he would be richly rewarded were he to choose magnificent Inverewe.

Magnolia x soulangeana

JANE WELSH CARLYLE HOUSE GARDEN, Haddington

Owner: The Lamp of Lothian Collegiate Trust

Off A1 Edinburgh to Dunbar road at Haddington

1400 hours to 1700 hours Wednesday to Saturday from April to September

The house in which Jane Welsh Carlyle was born was built in 1797 in what is now Lodge Street, Haddington. Originally, there were two houses known as 'the fore-tenement and the rear-tenement' which were 'linked by a building containing domestic offices', pulled down when the Carlyle House (as it is now known) was restored by the local charitable organization, Lamp of Lothian, in 1962. In 1802, both properties were bought by a Haddington writer (lawyer), David Rochead, who sold the fore-tenement to Dr John Welsh, Jane's father, for £300. In 1806, Dr Welsh bought the rear-tenement, previously rented, for use as his surgery. The evidence suggests that Jane Welsh was born in 1801 in the rear-tenement before her father bought it.

While no plan of the garden as it was in Jane's day exists, we know that there was a pear-tree close to the house; that she loved flowers and took cuttings of sweet-briar to grow in her garden at Cheyne Row and that when she revisited the Haddington garden in 1844, the Howden family, who then owned the house, brought her a bunch of flowers from her 'own garden'.

The small garden, now laid out according to the fashion of her time, and using only plants available early in the 19th century, is formal in design, having two main lawns bissected by a pathway and box-edged borders. Under the containing walls, against which plum trees have been planted, there are further borders. The rear of the house facing the garden is hung with roses and wisteria and two slender birch trees dominate the far end. The beds contain the old-fashioned flowers one would expect. Amongst others are astrantia, lavender, honeysuckle, jasmine, santolina, valerian and paeonies.

KAILZIE, near Peebles

Owner: Lady Angela Buchan-Hepburn

2½ miles from Peebles town centre on B7062 road to Traquair

Gardens only open all year round. Otherwise season is from end of March to end of October

The estate of Kailzie — 'valley of trees' — is an extensive one. The plain early Victorian house was occupied by the Richards family from 1914 to 1962, when it was de-roofed to avoid payment of rates — one of the most damaging pieces of rate-saving legislation ever enacted from the heritage point of view, since it resulted in the loss of many fine buildings so treated — and, inevitably, shortly after, demolished. There are two impressive little lodges at the entrance from the Peebles–Traquair road, a stable block dating from 1811 and a much earlier doocot. There is a shop and restaurant in the farm block and also a stocked fishing pond. The gardens cover some 18 acres of wild and formal areas.

During World War II, the impressive Walled Garden was laid out to grass, but is now beautifully planted with shrubs in great variety, including the magnificent *Cotinus coggygria* 'Royal Purple' which combines with the autumnal shades of berberis. There are shrub roses as well as a small formal rose garden, where a statue of Mercury seems to be pointing to another of a woman, set in an arch over which leylandii trees are being trained as a framework. There are several sections, intersected by grass, to the garden, the central one of which contains a double herbaceous border, ablaze with phlox, anthemis and the rich hues of heleniums. This end is marked by a sundial. Towards the upper section, there is a Laburnum alley, which drips gloriously yellow in spring.

As is customary, vegetable plots live happily as neighbours with the flowers. Huge Kelsae onions, traditionally sown on Christmas or Boxing Day, (as if one did not have enough to do then!), hobnob with a nearby block of vibrant pink mallows. The large and productive greenhouses contain, on the walls, peaches and figs as well as a splendid collection of fuchsias at their exhibition-best in June.

Outside the Walled Garden, there is a large woodland area of 15 acres dominated by magnificent specimen trees such as, allegedly, the largest larch in Scotland and a proud Blue abies whose characteristically drooping branches sweep down to the ground. In spring, this part of the garden, through which a burn runs, is carpeted with snowdrops, daffodils and meconopses, the Himalayan blue poppy, and enormous blocks of rhododendrons and azaleas.

Even the high walls provide their own colour. The ever-spreading pink *Erinus alpinus* and toadflax luxuriate in the seemingly impossibly small nooks and crannies. Peacocks are an added attraction and visitors are not mistaken if they catch sight of amber eyes staring fixedly at them from their perch among the leaves. Two Iranian eagle owls are the culprits.

Laburnum

KELLIE CASTLE

Owner: The National Trust for Scotland
On B9171, 3 miles north-north-west of Pittenweem
April to September from dawn to dusk

Kellie Castle, on the south side of Kellie Law, originally stood on land owned by the Sewards, who in about 1600 sold it to Thomas Erskine, later the 1st Earl of Mar and Kellie. The oldest part of the castle dates from 1360, but most of it dates from about 1606. Abandoned early in the 19th century, it was bought by Professor James Lorimer in 1878. His 16-year-old son, Robert, later Sir Robert, the famous Scottish architect, drew up his plan for the garden in 1880 and for the kitchen garden in 1884. Kellie Castle became his home. His idea was to recreate the atmosphere of the traditional 'cottage garden'—fruit, flowers and vegetables growing together—an aim continued in the later restoration of Sir Robert's sculptor son, Hew, and his wife and by the National Trust for Scotland, for whom the castle and 16 acres of surrounding land were bought in 1970 with a grant from the Secretary of State for Scotland, some assistance from the Pilgrim Trust, and financial help from an anonymous Trust member.

The Trust's restoration was helped by notes which Gertrude Jekyll made when she visited Kellie late in the 19th century. The pattern for the main borders has been based on an illustrated article about Kellie Castle which appeared in *Country Life* in July 1906.

The garden as a whole is divided into four sections by hedges and walks, with a sundial as its centre point. The first view leads the visitor towards the main herbaceous border, which is particularly lovely during July and August, when helenium and sidalcea are in full bloom. The path leads to an arch of 'Dorothy Perkins' ramblers. Another path, which converges in the centre, is lined with splendid specimens of versicoloured *Rosa gallica*.

In the south-west corner, a small 'secret garden' (for obvious reasons known as 'Robin's Garden'), is surrounded by a trellis over which climbing roses and hybrid clematis clamber.

Penstemon and erigeron line one side of another path, 'Peace' roses the other. Behind it, white clematis bloom in profusion and a vigorous honeysuckle throws over it all its canopy of perfume.

In the north-west corner, there is a garden house designed by Sir Robert which is topped on the roof by a small stone monkey.

Pink and white paeonies, a favourite in Scottish gardens, are much in evidence and are at their peak during May, as well as roses especially selected for their perfume, as are such old-fashioned favourites as Sweet William.

As the National Trust for Scotland claims, the underlying charm of the garden at Kellie is the 'apparently controlled disorder of the plants, which seems to flow from the borders contained only by immaculately maintained hedges of box'. It is, indeed, an 'everyone's kind of garden', which some think to be at its best in August.

The Victorian novelist Mrs Margaret Oliphant set one of her tales, *Katy Stewart,* in the castle.

Rosa 'PEACE'

KILDRUMMY CASTLE GARDENS, Kildrummy

Owner: Kildrummy Castle Gardens Trust

On A97, off A944 at Kildrummy

Daily from 1000 hours to 1700 hours
from April to October

Ancient Kildrummy Castle stood on a rocky eminence between two ravines. It was once a seat of the
kings of Scotland. Captured by Edward I of England
in 1306, early in the 14th century it passed to the
Earls of Mar and is supposed to have been the seat
of much of the planning for the 1715 Jacobite Rising,
an event which cost Mar the ownership of it. By
then, however, it must have been in a much reduced
state, for it was severely damaged by Cromwell. In
1731, the Gordons of Beldornie and Wardhouse
bought the estate. They and their descendants
planted Silver firs, larches and Hemlock spruce
around the den.

In 1898 a soap manufacturer, Colonel James Ogston,
acquired it. He built the English Tudor-style house
which replaced the old Gordon Lodge. Known as the
'new castle', it is now a hotel.

The trees planted by the Gordon owners formed a
shelter belt which proved useful when, with the help of
Japanese landscape gardeners, the Ogstons established
a water garden, making use of the Burn of Backden.
Here, moisture-loving plants such as hostas, veratrum,
ligularia and *Lysichitum americanus* flourish. The solid
arch of the entrance bridge, said to be a replica of the
'Brig o' Balgownie' near Aberdeen, is reflected in the
quiet waters below, and through it there is a fine view of
the shrubs further up. The lower reaches of the ancient
sandstone quarry in the den provided an excellent
location for the alpine garden, constructed by Back-
houses of York in 1904. Here, surrounding the immaculate lawn, little paths meander through the boulders
and steps. Temperatures even in May are very low
(Kildrummy lies on a latitude north of Moscow!), but it
is quite remarkable how many tender species continue
to grow and proliferate, thanks to the care lavished
upon them.

Falkland Palace   *Virginia creeper*   *page 97*

Threave House   *daffodils*   *page 185*

Dawyck Botanic Garden   *snowdrops near Swiss bridge*   page 80

Kellie Castle   page 132
delphinium border and sundial

General Ogston succeeded his brother at Kildrummy and continued developing the garden. He also established a collection of old millstones, Pictish stones and other exhibits, now housed in a museum.

The high side of the den gives some protection from the winds that sweep the north-east in winter, but frost and snow bring problems and over the years some valuable plantings have been lost. There is, therefore, no attempt at formality at Kildrummy, plants being placed (wisely) where they have the best chance of survival. The 'Norquinco Valley' form of embothrium does continue to flame up the wall and has proved quite hardy, despite late frosts. On the other hand, *Spiraea douglasii* has become an almost ineradicable weed.

Kildrummy's interesting trees include a lovely *Acer japonicum* 'Aurea', a sturdy purple oak and, most interesting of all, a weeping hemlock. It resulted as a cross between two species and is unique to Kildrummy.

KILMORY CASTLE, Lochgilphead

Owner: Argyll and Bute District Council

Right off A83 Inverary to Lochgilphead road immediately before the town

Daily throughout the year

Kilmory, from the Gaelic 'Cille Mhoire', St Mary's Chapel, the site of which still exists in the grounds, was for generations owned by the Campbells, the last of whom died in the 1820s, leaving a daughter, Eliza, who married Sir John Powlett Orde. He commissioned the London architect J G Davis to pull down the old house and build the present mansion in what might be called 'Sir Walter Scott Gothic'. Between 1828 and 1878, when he died, he wrought vast improvements.

He commissioned Sir William Hooker in 1830 to lay out the grounds, basing his arrangements on the original garden, dating from the 1770s. Hooker, at that time Professor of Botany at Glasgow University, but later Director of Kew Gardens, planted many exotic trees. The collections of hardy ferns and alpines were said at one time to rival those in Edinburgh's Royal Botanic Garden. Some of the plants still to be seen at Kew were, in fact, propagated at Kilmory. There was also a fine, formal walled garden.

In 1938, however, the estate was sold by the Orde family. Under a succession of owners the gardens and grounds fell into neglect and were in just such a state of disrepair when fortunately, in 1974, Argyll County Council (later to be the Argyll and Bute District Council) bought Kilmory.

Most cared-for gardens do not stand still — plants are changed; borders replanted, in even the smallest of plots. Kilmory gardens are no exception. Mervyn Kessell and his assistant Alison MacIlroy are ever eager to create yet another garden; yet another vista. Plans are afoot, for instance, to redesign the woodland and wild garden, but to retain, of course, the healthy, mature trees in which this area is particularly rich. Already the two of them have created a herb garden, Memorial Garden (to the memory of Ken Beckwith, a fine gardener, who was much concerned with the re-development at Kilmory), a pond and a herbaceous border. Many specimen trees and shrubs have also been added to a garden which fortunately retains much of the original planting. Another worthwhile aim is to have as many plants as possible clearly named and a considerable start to this has already been made.

As one would expect, Kilmory is rich in venerable rhododendrons thanks to the sympathetic growing conditions. The Hooker seed was shared widely throughout west-coast Scotland and here you will find, amongst many others, magnificent specimens of *R falconeri, grande, arboreum, campanulatum, cinnabarinum, luteum* and *davidsonianum*, as well as hybrids like 'Elizabeth', 'Lord Roberts', 'Saltire', 'Songbird' and a host of others. To date, also happily flourishing are 18 varieties of azalea which range from 'Liliput' to 'Everest' and 'Princess Anne' to 'Princess Juliana'.

Within the last 10 years an enormous number of trees and shrubs has been added, too many to be listed, but including a variety of acers (two of the negundo form—'elegans' and 'variegatum'), a golden Indian Bean Tree, *Catalpa Bignonioides* 'Aurea', varieties of maple and buddleia (to encourage butterflies), a Judas Tree, *Cercis siliquastrum*, usually somewhat tender in other parts of Scotland, and a Tulip tree, *Liliodendron tulipifera*. Perhaps the most interesting of all is a sturdy *Sciadopitys verticillata*, the Japanese umbrella pine.

In spring, the Walled Garden is ablaze with colour. Carpeting the azaleas and rhododendrons are glorious mounds of moss, an inspired combination of fresh green and vibrant shades.

The Council were fortunate in inheriting many splendid trees which still thrived despite the rapid degeneration which normally occurs in a garden which has been neglected over a period of years. There is, for instance, a magnificent *Cryptomeria japonica*, one of the tallest in the country, an equally splendid *Crinodendron hookerianum*, and a fine *Cercidiphyllum japonicum*. There are also Western red cedars, Sitka spruce, Western hemlock and many more.

A future ambition is that Kilmory should house the National Collection of Ferns, the basis of which already exists.

While most garden furniture ultimately gives out, that at Kilmory is not likely to — it is made of stone! Some new, finely-executed wrought-iron gates, commissioned locally, have been installed.

Much loving care and considerable effort has gone into making Kilmory the fine garden it already is. It is one whose progress will be watched with interest and is well worth a visit.

KINROSS HOUSE

Owner: Sir David Montgomery Bt

½ mile from Kinross

May to September

Kinross House, one of the earliest triumphs of early classical Scottish architecture, was built by Sir William Bruce, friend and confidant of Charles II, and architect of the later sections of Holyroodhouse. It became the seat of the Grahams of Kinross in the 18th century and passed by marriage to Sir Graham Graham Montgomery in 1816, from whom the present owner descends. Because it lay empty during much of the 19th century, it was spared Victorian alteration.

The gardens, located on the far side, are laid out in the grand manner, and are said to have cost Sir William Bruce more than £400 a year to maintain — an enormous sum in the 17th century! After neglect while the house was not occupied, they were laid out again in the original manner by Sir Basil Montgomery in 1902.

The garden, walled on all sides, has long herbaceous borders, rose beds, wide lawns and yew hedges, enhanced by statues and stone summerhouses, and a central fountain. It is a garden with superb vistas. From the Fish Gate, there is a splendid view of the great house with the fountain intervening (the house, incidentally, thought by Daniel Defoe to be 'the most beautiful and regular piece of architecture in Scotland', and by the historian, Sir Robert Sibbald as 'unsurpassed by few in the country'). Looking the other way, the view is towards Loch Leven and Castle Island, where Mary, Queen of Scots was imprisoned in 1567–8. She escaped on 2 May 1568 and embarked on the chain of events that led to defeat at the Battle of Langside, the flight to England, 18 years of incarceration at Fotheringay and eventual execution on the orders of Elizabeth I. It is a truly romantic garden.

LITTLE SPARTA, Dunsyre

Owners: Ian Hamilton Finlay and Sue Finlay

Off the A702 at Dolphinton, along the Dolphinton to Newbigging road, about 1 mile beyond Dunsyre

Only by arrangement (Telephone: 089 981 252)

Little Sparta stands at the southern end of the Pentland Hills and is reached by a long and rough stony path (with two farm gates to be opened and closed), high on reclaimed moorland. Twenty-five years ago, Ian Hamilton Finlay took over a little farm with only one tree, and on five acres of ground proceeded to create a garden that has attracted international interest. He was by then already known as a poet, his *Glasgow Beasts* Scots sequence moving towards the realms of 'concrete verse', then becoming fashionable in Scotland. His garden creations are, in fact, an extension of his poetry; as if the poet had looked again at the very point and purpose of the gardener's art with fresh eyes. So original and beautiful, indeed, were the results that they soon began to attract universal attention.

Not surprisingly, he regards Little Sparta as his most important achievement, although he has created sections of garden in gardens and parks in other countries, notably Holland and Germany. He also created a remarkable garden at Glasgow's Garden Festival in 1990; a stony path with a stile, surrounded by a rich variety of grasses.

His, then, is an imaginative and poetic reinterpretation of an old tradition. The idea of using buildings or sculpture in gardens goes back a long way. In the mid 19th century, however, J C Loudon's 'Gardenesque' (as he called it) policy of concentrating on the plants themselves rather drove the older idea out of favour. What Ian Hamilton Finlay has done is to revive the classical tradition in which garden buildings, plants, water (especially water) and landscape merge to create a general effect, yet also retain their own identities.

Little Sparta is exposed and windswept, with fairly thin acidic soil. Finlay himself says that the Pentlands winter is long, with spring slow in coming and short in stay. The growing time is therefore from June to September.

The garden is made up of a number of themed 'rooms', each leading to the next and each containing an inserted slab or sculpted object. To the south of the house is a Roman Garden. There are no busts of gods and goddesses here, or, indeed, in most of the other 'rooms'. One 'room' does, in fact, house APOLLON TERRORISTE, a large gold helmeted head set in the woodland near one of the pools; but today it is tanks, aircraft and submarines that wield power, not the old gods and goddesses. Thus, down a path arched over by honeysuckle and flanked by foxgloves, irises and currant bushes, two bronze tortoises emerge out of potentilla with 'Panzer Leader' engraved across their shells. Elsewhere, there is an aircraft carrier with a bird-bath on the landing deck and an ornamental submarine. The Henry Vaughan Walk contains three square columns carrying words from an essay by the Silurist poet Henry Vaughan: 'The contemplation of death is an obscure melancholy walk . . . an expiation in shadows and solitude . . . but it leads unto life.' Finlay's sardonic humour is frequently evident—a group of wild cherry trees is fronted by a tombstone bearing the inscription: 'Bring back the Birch'.

The sunken garden, immediately in front of the house and the first to be developed, is paved with inscribed slabs, surrounded by the subtle colours of astrantia and ferns—indeed, all the colours in this remarkable garden are muted. In front of this garden there is a table-like sundial wreathed by a currant bush. The neighbouring fruit garden has tall raspberry canes punctuated by stakes painted at random in pink and deep red stripes, both decorative and useful as supports.

On the opposite side of the path is the Pompeiian Garden. Here, small fluted columns rise out of careful groupings of campanula, spiraea, dog-rose and astilbe. In its small circular pool a blue glass fishing-net float drifts, shifting before the wind and carrying the observation: 'The sphere complements the circle.' The terrace garden has *Rosa rugosa* framing inscribed slabs, memorials to lost ships.

To the left of the front garden, between the side of the house and at right angles to the gable of one of the garden workshops (covered by an espalier cherry tree), is Julie's Garden, named after the heroine of one of Jean Jacques Rousseau's novels. The other three sides of this little 'room' are surrounded by conifers. A brick path winds through gooseberries, apples, currant bushes, foxgloves and rowan trees, each carrying an inscribed ceramic plaque.

Behind the house is the Temple Pool (fringed with Goat willows, rowans, mimulus and floating water-lilies), which contains a marble boat on a column. A lawn edged with capitals (as if the rest of the columns lay buried) fronts the temple itself.

To the north-west is the woodland garden, which features a large pyramid dedicated to the Romantic German painter, Caspar David Friedrich, in front of sombre conifers and two large cut-outs of Apollo and Daphne.

The gloom here contrasts with the heathery hillside area beyond, whose major feature is the small Lochan Eck. Overlooking it are several, apparently casually 'dropped', hewn stones bearing the warning message: 'The Present Order is the Disaster of the Future', a prophecy uttered by the French revolutionary Saint-Just, himself commemorated by an impressive single column arising out of the waters of the lochan. Near its edge there also emerges the conning tower of a nuclear submarine, inscribed: 'Nuclear Sail', the common nautical term for the superstructure on such boats. In striking contrast, two graceful black swans slip quietly across the water and in among the bullrushes.

The Hegel stile, further up the hill, is inscribed: 'THESIS: fence, ANTITHESIS: gate, SYNTHESIS: stile.' Around the upper pool, amidst alders, poplars, spruce and wild cherry, we are urged to: 'See Pousin, Hear Lorrain'.

It is impossible in this brief context to describe all the

surprises this hugely original garden affords. It really
has to be seen. The philosophy behind it, however, is
best encompassed by Finlay's *Detached Sentences of
Gardening*, some of which assert:

> Classic gardens are composed of Glooms and Soli-
> tudes and not of plants and trees.
> In modern gardens a bench is a thing to be sat upon;
> in William Shenstone's garden (The Leasowes) it was a
> thing to be read.
> Horticulturalists enter the neo-classical garden with
> the air of Police conducting a weapon search.
> Certain gardens are described as retreats when they
> are really attacks.

A plan of the layout of the garden is made available to
his visitors by the genial Ian Hamilton Finlay.

LOCHINCH AND CASTLE KENNEDY, by Stranraer

Owners: The Earl and Countess of Stair

4 miles east of Stranraer on A75 Stranraer to Dumfries road, signposted at Castle Kennedy village

1 April or Easter weekend to end of September daily from 1000 hours to 1700 hours

Castle Kennedy was once the seat of the Kennedys, who obtained their first charter to the lands in the 14th century. John, Lord Kennedy, was appointed Keeper of the Manor Place and Loch of Inch in 1482. The old castle, built by John, 5th Earl of Cassillis in 1609, was accidentally destroyed by fire in 1716 and never restored, though the walls are still standing. Castle Kennedy was eventually replaced in 1864 by Lochinch Castle at the other end of the estate (which covers 75 acres in all), a Scottish Baronial edifice with pepper-pot turrets and corbie-stepped gables. The sunken garden alongside it was probably created at the same time.

That enthusiastic writer on gardens, Sir Herbert Maxwell, in his *Scottish Gardens*, written in 1908 — incidentally, how many of the great gardens described by him a century ago are now no more! — picturesquely set the scene:

Here, on the isthmus between two seas, lie two ample sheets of fresh water, the Black and White Lochs of Inch; and the inner isthmus between these lakes has been wrought into a strange complexity of terraces and grassy slopes. The ruins of Castle Kennedy stand on one end of this isthmus. At the other end, the best part of a mile distant, is the modern mansion of Lochinch, residence of the Earl of Stair, a spacious specimen of that style which was developed under French influence in the sixteenth century, when country houses, ceasing to be purely defensive, assumed more hospitable features.

The gardens were laid out between 1730 and 1740 by John, 2nd Earl of Stair and a field marshal, victor of Dettingen, who had also been British ambassador to France and was much influenced by the grandeur and graciousness of Versailles. While he was abroad, his gardener, Thomas M'Allan, kept him informed of

144

progress by letter, reporting on 29 January 1737, for example: 'I have ben Removing the tris out of the gret land belo the belvadair . . . I humbly thank your lordshep for the gret Incuregen leter I got. It was very Inlivening and reviving to me.'

Mr M'Allan had the assistance of the Royal Scots Grays and the Inniskillen Fusiliers, along with their horses, to implement his master's plans, which included an area of military terracing, now grass-covered.

'The tris', the planting of which cost M'Allan so much conscientious effort, were, however, laid low and sold for timber by the 7th Earl (known as 'Hobblin' Jock' because he walked with a limp), who also allowed the gardens to return to their natural state. In 1840, his heir, the 8th Earl, discovered the plan of the original layout of the garden in a gardener's cottage and set about restoring things. He added a collection of exotic conifers, still to be seen today, as well as many other rare trees and shrubs.

The layout of the garden is spacious. A driveway from the A75 leads round the Black Loch to the garden entrance. Ahead lies the gaunt, ruined shape of Castle Kennedy, which must have been commodious by the standards of the day, as well as defensively secure. To the right, a great expanse, including the folds of the grassy ramparts, stretches down to the lily pond (the surface of which is almost completely solid with water-lilies), with the White Loch beyond. Round the pond there are clumps of azaleas and rhododendrons, and in the borders bold masses of agapanthus, crocosmia and orange lilies. To the left of the old castle is the walled garden. Its central herbaceous border contains both shrubs and perennials. Buddleias and berberis blend with fuchsias, penstemons in various colours and bright red geraniums. An *Echium pininana*, acanthus, and tall *Macleaya microcarpa* dominate another border. A fine griselinia overlooks the wall nearest the old castle, and immediately inside the gate a brilliant *Callistemon citrinus* adds colour to the high wall behind it.

The broad path down the slope towards the White Loch, known as Dettingen Avenue, has many mature Ilexes with an inner avenue of embothriums, alternating with magnificent specimens of *Eucryphia glutinosa*.

All the paths and avenues, 'like spokes of a giant wheel', as one commentator put it, converge on the circular lily pond. One such spectacular avenue is made up of *Araucaria araucana*, or Monkey Puzzle, now a century old and over 70 feet tall, with azaleas along either side.

Despite these attractions, the outstanding feature of the garden is its collection of rhododendrons, some more than a century old, such as *Rhododendron arboreum*, grown from Himalayan seed brought back by Sir Joseph Hooker. The mild, damp climate prevailing in south-west Scotland here as elsewhere suits them well. Other flowering shrubs include magnolias and camellias.

This must be one of the largest gardens in Scotland, and amply repays the visitor who has the time and energy to walk all round it.

Araucaria araucana

LOGAN BOTANIC GARDEN, Port Logan, Stranraer

Owner: Royal Botanic Garden Edinburgh

14 miles south of Stranraer on B7065

15 March to 31 October daily from 1000 hours to 1800 hours and other times by special arrangement

Logan Botanic Garden lies between two expanses of water, Luce Bay on the east and the Irish Sea on the west, almost at the southern tip of the Rhinns of Galloway and thus of Scotland. Effectively, it therefore has sea water on three sides, the peninsula being only about two miles broad at Logan. While it suffers from salt-laden gales, from which a modern belt of *Pittosporum, Griselinia, Olearia* and *Phormium* now protects it, it otherwise enjoys a relatively beneficent climate as a result of the flow of the Gulf Stream. Indeed, it has been compared, in horticultural terms, to the climate experienced by the Scilly Isles. As a result, plants from the southern hemisphere thrive here. In fact, most of the collections of the Royal Botanic Garden Edinburgh from southern South America, southern Africa and Australasia are now located at Logan. Another advantage is the soil, a slightly acid loam, ideally suited for rhododendrons, camellias and several montane species which thrive in moist, peaty conditions. The rainfall (40 inches annually), as summer holiday-makers sometimes discover to their disadvantage, is more or less evenly distributed throughout the year, no one month being conspicuously the wettest.

John Baliol, Lord of Galloway, gave Logan—or Lougan, as it was then called—to Dougal McDouall in 1295. The McDoualls' first home was the Castle of Balzieland, burnt down in 1500, although a tall surviving fragment is now dramatically incorporated in the west wall, above the terrace overlooking the walled garden. The estate came down through generations, father to son, until 1945, when Kenneth McDouall left Logan to his cousin, Sir Ninian Buchan-Hepburn. In 1949, the estate passed into the ownership of Mr R Olaf Hambro, himself an enthusiastic and knowledgeable gardener, whose trustees made over the garden to the nation in 1969, at which time the house—basically early 18th century—and the rest of the estate were reacquired by Sir Ninian. The garden, however, became a Specialist Garden of the Royal Botanic Garden Edinburgh.

It appears that there probably was a garden on the site from medieval times, growing fruit and vegetables. The present garden stems from 1869, when James McDouall married Agnes Buchan-Hepburn (Sir Ninian's great-aunt). She was a keen gardener and planted lilies, roses and shrubs, which she brought with her from the garden of the East Lothian house in which she had been reared. She also planted the first eucalyptus trees. She had two sons, both keen and knowledgeable gardeners, Kenneth, the last McDouall laird, and his brother Douglas, both of whom travelled widely in warm temperate regions to collect their own new species, as well as obtain seed from such famous contemporary plant-collectors as George Forrest, Reginald Farrer and others. The fruit and vegetable garden was thus transformed into today's home of rare and exotic plants.

In 1909, the McDouall brothers planted an avenue of over 60 little Cabbage palms, *Cordyline australis*, which they had grown from seed. These—or rather their successors, also grown from seed, the originals having suffered severely in the gales of 1963—are one of the first sights that greet today's visitor as he or she passes through the entrance. The brothers were also responsible for the *Trachycarpus fortunei*, or Chusan Palm, on both sides of the burn flowing from Deer Hill, through the mightily thriving Gunnera Bog—home to the largest *Gunnera manicata* in Scotland, it is said— towards the entrance. Another feature, planted some 70 years ago, is the evergreen Tree fern, *Dicksonia antarctica*, magnificent specimens of which can be found in the walled garden.

It is obviously not possible to deal in minute detail with the many thousands of rare trees, shrubs and plants to be found at Logan. (A detailed examination of these, along with the contents of the Royal Botanic Garden Edinburgh and those of the other Specialist Gardens at Benmore and Dawyck, can be found in

4 Gardens in One, by Deni Bown, published by the Royal Botanic Garden.) We must therefore content ourselves with describing the layout of this wonderful and remarkable garden, and indicating some of the principal seasonal attractions.

Through the wooded entrance and past other administrative buildings, the visitor on turning right comes to the water garden and the Tree ferns, beyond which is the middle walled garden with, above it, the terrace. To the right of the water garden is the peat wall garden. The McDouall brothers were Scottish pioneers in the development of the peat walled garden—an experiment stimulated by the need to provide favourable conditions for plants from China and the Himalayas that require constant moisture and humidity but also good drainage and acid soil, conditions not found in the drier traditional rock garden—though in their early experiments at Logan they used turves. In more recent years the same technique has been widely employed both in the Royal Botanic Garden Edinburgh and at Branklyn, Perth. Here at Logan, the peat wall garden hosts alpines and other lime-hostile plants. Beyond it lies the lower walled garden. To the north of the Castle Balzieland ruin lies the castle woodland.

To the left of the visitors' reception area and shop lies the south woodland, beyond which is the Gunnera Bog and, outwith the garden's formal bounds, Deer Hill.

As in so many Scottish gardens, daffodils make a spring display at Logan, here to be found beneath the Chusan palms, an interesting combination of the familiar and the rare. These are followed by the flowering of many rhododendrons and magnolias. Among the rhododendrons that thrive at Logan but only occasionally elsewhere in Scotland are *R maddenii*, and the best known of its hybrids, 'Fragrantissimum'; *R edgeworthii*; the equally well-scented *R formosum*, and the scentless *R ciliatum*.

Among the magnolias are *M sprengeri*, in the lower walled garden, and *M campbellii*, or giant Himalayan Tulip tree, magnificent in height and beauty.

Camellias, as would be expected, do well at Logan.

They are to be found on the north side of the central wall between the walled gardens; notably *C japonica*, *C reticulata* and *C saluenensis*, as well as the north Chinese *C cuspidata* and the East Asian *C oleifera*.

Skunk cabbages, the large-leafed *Lysichiton americanus* and *L camtschatcensis*, together with Arum lilies, *Zantedeschia*, and the Water hawthorn, *Aponogeton distachyus*, adorn the water garden in spring, presided over in summer by Cabbage palms, *Cordyline australis*, curiously named since their leaves are really sword shaped.

In summer, too, the flower beds in the walled garden are at their most brilliant. The display includes salvias—red, *S gesnerifolia*; pink, *S neurepia*; blue *S semiatrata* and *S ambigens*. Of the bedding plants, six or seven thousand are used every year. There are also larger-growing perennials like the lovely 'Angels' Fishing-rods', *Dierama pulcherrimum*, and various members of the iris family, including the eye-catching scarlet *Crocosmia* 'Lucifer'.

Blue African lilies, *Agapanthus*, are to be seen; and the red brush-like *Callistemon rigidus*, up against the centre wall. Dahlias, too, flourish, including the largest of the species, *D imperialis* and *D merckii* and also the hardy 'Bishop of Llandaff', as well as that intriguing relative of the dahlia family, *Cosmos atrosanguineus* with its smell of rich chocolate. Spectacular, too, is the orange-star (but stinging-haired) *Blumenbachia acanthifolia* and the many varieties of fuchsia, including *F arborescens*, the Mexican *F microphylla* and the hardiest and most common, *F magellanica*, which is seen all over the west of Scotland. Particularly striking is the New Zealand *Fuchsia excorticata*, the purple-green flower of which grows directly from the bark. Also from New Zealand, incidentally, is the scarlet fiery-pointed 'Christmas Tree', *Metrosideros umbellata*, in the middle walled garden.

Add, in spring, the primula-scattered path leading from the garden to the Port Logan fish pond, late flowerers like the Trumpet-creeper, *Campsis radicans*, the delicate crinum, *C moorei* from southern Africa, the many grasses, flaxes and rare-barked trees, like the Mount Wellington peppermint, *Eucalyptus coccifera*, and *Polylepis australis*, a member of the Rosaceae family, originally from Argentina, and it is obvious that Logan Botanic Garden, a clearly labelled delight to the non-technical garden lover, at all seasons is an absolute 'must' on the Scottish visiting-list of the serious plantsman, second only perhaps to the parent Royal Botanic Garden Edinburgh, though a very close second.

MALLENY GARDEN

Owner: The National Trust for Scotland
8 miles from Edinburgh on A70. Turn off at Balerno
Daily all year round from 1000 hours to sunset

Malleny House was owned by the Knychtsoune family from 1478 to 1617, when it was sold, changing hands several times until 1647, when it was bought by William Scott. It stayed with the Scotts until 1882, when Sir Francis Cunningham Scott sold it to the 5th Earl of Rosebery. It was then leased to a succession of tenants—one of whom, Sir Thomas Gibson-Carmichael, was responsible for much fine wrought-iron work, not all of it still at Malleny. In 1960, Malleny was bought by Commander and Mrs Gore-Browne Henderson who, in 1968, presented it to the National Trust for Scotland. The house, which has an 1810 Georgian addition, is not open to the public.

The wind vane represents the yacht *Jullanar*, something of a design-prototype when built in Essex in 1875. The dovecot has, unusually, a saddleback roof. The figure on the roof and the Rosebery coat of arms were designed by Sir Thomas, but the wrought-iron entrance gate is the work of Schomberg Scott.

The garden covers nine acres in all, seven of them woodland and two a three-sided walled garden. Of the twelve clipped yews planted in 1603—the 'Twelve Apostles', they were dubbed—eight were cut down by Mrs Gore-Brown Henderson because they excluded light from the 1810 addition.

The garden, entered through the wrought-iron gate, is divided at right angles roughly in half by a *Taxus baccata* (yew) hedge. The central path from the entrance gates runs through an archway to the middle of the wall in the lower garden, thus dividing it into four.

From the entrance (before passing the four yew trees) the path to the left leads to the house. That to the right passes through mixed borders to the area where the collection of bonsai (established in 1988 by the Scottish Bonsai Society) is kept in an electronically protected wire-meshed enclosure. Among the 50 or so varieties here are *Buddleia davidii, nothofagus* and *larix*. One container holds a 'miniature forest' of Scots pine.

Malleny also has a national collection of 19th-century roses, which it holds for the National Council for the Conservation of Plants and Gardens. They grow in the borders and about the boundary paths, as well as in the south-east quarter of the garden — 140 cultivars in all, including the Gallica roses 'Belle de Crécy' and 'Tuscany'. Here, too, are 'Empress Josephine', 'Portland Rose' and 'Blanc Doubie de Coubert' among very many others.

But such specialities apart, there is a wide range of other delights to be seen in this high-summer scented garden, including *Geranium renardii, G macrorrhizum* 'Album', *Salix lanata, Lychnis viscaria, Erigeron mucronatus, Polygonum affine* and, in the border nearest the house, delphiniums, paeonies, hollyhocks and the Burnet rose, *Rosa pimpinellifolia*.

In the north-east corner of the garden there is a vegetable and herb garden, the herbs being enclosed in triangular beds bounded by stone setts.

MANDERSTON, Duns

Owners: Lord and Lady Palmer

2 miles east of Duns on A6105

6 May to 30 September, Thursdays and Saturdays, from 1400 hours to 1730 hours. Also Bank Holiday Mondays. Parties (minimum 20) by arrangement at any time of the year

Manderston is Scotland's finest monument to Edwardian opulence, in spite of its deliberate neo-Georgian quality. The original house on the site, built in 1790 by either Alexander Gilbie or John White, was commissioned by Dalhousie Weatherstone. In 1855, the estate was bought by Richard Miller. On his death it was acquired by his younger brother, great-great-great-grandfather of the present owner. Miller had made his fortune trading hemp and herrings with the Russians and, indeed, was Honorary British Consul at St Petersburg for 16 years. He returned to become Liberal Member of Parliament, first for Leith and then for Berwickshire. Although it is said that he never spoke a word in the House, on the strength of his political dinners the Prime Minister, William Gladstone, successfully recommended his elevation to a Baronetcy in 1874.

Sir William found the Georgian house too old-fashioned for his taste, so had the architect, James Simpson, carry out various modernizing improvements. His heir-intended, a schoolboy at Eton, died choking on a cherry stone, and the title and the estate therefore went to his second son, Sir James Miller, said to have been 'the perfect Edwardian gentleman'. He married the Honourable Eveline Curzon, daughter of Lord Scarsdale, whose home, Kedleston Hall in Derbyshire, was one of Robert Adam's masterpieces. No doubt anxious to impress his father-in-law, between 1894 and 1900 Sir James had the architect John Kinross build a boathouse by the lake in the form of an Alpine chalet and the Georgian-style stable block, game-keeper's cottage and kennels. Then Sir James went off to the Boer War. In 1901, on his return, he commissioned Kinross to remodel Manderston, making it more spacious although adhering to the neo-Georgian manner, money being no object.

The policies extend to 56 acres. Four years after the house was finished, Sir James had Kinross set about the redesigning of the garden, leaving, however, the spacious lawns of 'Capability Brown'-style layout (among the few to survive in Scotland) to the north more or less unaltered.

The garden with four terraces to the south and east of the house is laid out formally. The uppermost terrace on the south side, with its views of the Cheviot Hills, contains plants of grey foliage, such as Lamb's Ear, *Staychis lanata* and *Lavandula spica* 'Hidcote', contrasting with the purple foliage of *Cotinus coggygria*. *Polygonum baldschuanicum* rambles up a flight of criss-cross steps. Pink hydrangeas, fuchsias and cotoneasters adorn the wall that drops down to the level of the main terrace, where two raised pools surround the statues of a nymph and a bronze sea-creature sprinkles water towards watching cherubs at the perimeter. The parterres are filled with red and yellow floribunda roses, bordered by variegated hostas and hollies and decked out with topiary yews. Beyond the south terraces, grass banks shelve down to a bed of rhododendrons by the lake, where a Chinese bridge-cum-dam at the east end leads to the walled garden.

On the east side, steps lead from a gateway flanked by gryphons to a descending terrace of mown grass, used for tennis and croquet. There are four impressive stone vases set equidistantly above the grass terrace. The eye-catching feature here is a handsome copper beech tree. The top border contains hostas and pink 'Cornelian' climbing roses.

The woodland garden was started in the 1950s by Major Bailie, the present owner's maternal grandfather, from whom he inherited the estate in 1978. Over the bridge-dam, there is a Japanese lantern and a pagoda, an odd oriental touch.

On a slope planted with Scots pine, larch, oak and cryptomeria, the Japanese cedar, there is a magnificent rhododendron collection, at its most colourful in May, which includes the late-flowering *R* 'Polar Bear', *R yunnanense* and *R hippophaeoides*. Other attractive specimens include *Daphne mezereum* 'grandiflora', shrub roses and trees with unusual barks such as *Betula jacquemontii*, *Prunus serrula* and *Acer griseum*. A summerhouse, a bronze heron and a Celtic-revival, circular seat are amongst the artefacts in this woody glade.

To the north of the house there is, in season, a spectacular display of daffodils among the huge trees, many of them dating from the original 18th-century garden. The grand gates leading to the formal garden are gilded so as to catch the rays of the setting sun and were brought to Manderston from a London house. Two central heart-shaped beds of begonias, fringed with alyssum and lobelia, set off a stone fountain. To one side lies a herbaceous border; to the other, a walk lined with dahlias and roses. Dividing the upper from the lower formal garden is a pergola covered with pink-flowering climbing roses, fronted by a plot of red bedding-plants. The lower garden has a well-head surrounded by stone urns filled with petunias and guarded by crouching lions. The bedding plants are changed regularly to maintain their colour. Further down are the unusual greenhouses, set at a lower level, their rock-face construction making them resemble a sunken garden. Ferns, fuchsias, pelargoniums and other plants are rooted in crannies in the rock. The Edwardian ironmongery is also of itself remarkable.

In Edwardian times, Manderston employed over 100 people. Today, it operates on eight full-time employees and the hard work of its owners. Yet it is more than remarkably well kept; a reminder, surely unique in Scotland, of that Elgarian world that vanished with the outbreak of World War I.

MELLERSTAIN, Gordon, Berwickshire

Owners: Lord and Lady Haddington

Off the A6089 south of Gordon

May to end September (except Saturday)
from 1230 hours to 1700 hours

Mellerstain was commissioned from William Adam by George Baillie of Jerviswood and Mellerstain and his wife, Lady Grizell (née Baillie), authoress of the Scots song *O Werena my Hert licht I Wad Die* and a *Household Book*, now a classic of its kind, invaluable as a social record of her age. One of her daughters, Rachel Baillie, married Charles, Lord Binning, eldest son of the 6th Earl of Haddington (whom he predeceased) in 1719. William Adam built the wings, but in the event it was his son Robert who built the central block for Lady Rachel's son, George, in 1778.

Throughout the late 18th and 19th centuries the house stood in a great swathe of parkland. The lake to the south was designed in the form of a Dutch canal when George Baillie, a Royalist who took refuge in Holland during the Cromwellian interlude, returned home.

The present lake, nevertheless, forms part of Sir Reginald Blomfield's design for the garden, which he carried out in 1909 for the 11th Earl of Haddington. The terrace gardens to the back of the house consist of a double balustraded descending staircase, leading to two large formal plots of segmented design, contained within a balustraded wall. In the centre, two stairways wind round a circular balustrade where, beyond the statue, the large wall-enclosed lawn leads to the distant lake, surrounded by trees, and, as a backdrop, a prospect of the Cheviots. There are broad herbaceous borders beneath the terraced steps and two raised balustraded platforms at either end.

MONTEVIOT, near Jedburgh

Owner: Lothian Estates

4 miles north of Jedburgh, Roxburghshire, off A68 on to B6400 to Nisbet

April to August inclusive. Monday to Thursday from 1400 hours to 1700 hours
Other openings are detailed in **The Gardens of Scotland** *handbook*

Monteviot—or Mount Teviot, as it was originally known—a Lothian property, stands near the left bank of the River Teviot, at the southern base of Peniel Heugh. It is now a much added to Gothic-style edifice—its latest refurbishment the work of the architect Schomberg Scott, who was a grandson of the Marquis of Lothian—though it contains the nucleus of an 18th-century farmhouse. Except for a period during World War II, when it was used as a hospital, it has always been occupied as a home. It was at one time owned by the Elliots and occupied by Admiral Elliot, the son of Sir Gilbert Elliot of Minto. His daughter, Jean, the authoress of the better version of *The Flowers of the Forest*, wrote her song while overlooking the rolling Border landscape viewed from Monteviot, perhaps in the library. She died in the house. The oldest surviving part of the garden is the Herb Garden, now edged at the front with ground-covering *Rosa* 'Surrey'. It is sheltered on three sides by the library and bedrooms, but with an open southern aspect and splendid view.

The Herb Garden is thus a courtyard, its parterre of clipped box hedges containing a wide range of herbs including tarragon, thymes, rosemary and lovage. The centre-piece of this formal area is a sundial dating from the same time as this section of the house, the walls of which used to carry *Rosa* 'Albertine', but which has now been replaced with *R* 'Paul's Treasure' (a hybrid of *R* 'Kiftsgate' and *R* 'Buff Beauty'), and the mildew-resistant *R* 'Cecile Brunner'.

Down immaculate grass terraces lies the next oldest part of the garden, the Victorian Rose Garden, sheltered by a 10-foot-high wall with buttresses. Formal, of two-tiers, and of fairly recent re-planting, following an outburst of rose sickness, it contains a magnificent collection of more than 80 different varieties of Shrub and Hybrid Tea roses, including 'Stella Gray' and the Musk rose *Fedschenkoana*. These have been carefully selected to provide a graduated spectrum of colour. Andrew Simmons, the former Head Gardener, opened up 'windows' through the shrubs at the bottom to give spectacular views of the river and also to allow winter frost to escape from this lower-lying area.

The top terrace contains two arches carrying pink rambler roses with actinidia climbing the wall behind. Blue clematis clambers along the buttresses. The climbing roses at Monteviot are pruned early (from late July to mid-August) and after pruning provide what is almost an etching of stems up the high walls. Reaching down towards the lower terrace, there is an abundance of alyssum, aubretia and saxifrage.

Like the Rose Garden, the Arboretum dates from mid-Victorian times, when seed-collectors were bringing back specimens from all over the world. Here there is a wide range of conifers — some of the rarest in these islands — as well as of deciduous trees, including the beech, *Fagus sylvatica* 'Albovariegata', and the variegated oak, the rare *Quercus robur* 'Variegata'; the second largest Syrian juniper in Britain; from the Balkans, *Quercus frainetto*, otherwise known as Hungarian oak, and from Japan, the Hondo spruce, *Picea jezoensis var, hondoensis*. These, along with an enormous example of *Larix kaempferi*, survived the great storm in 1993. The Macedonian pine, over 90 feet high, said to be the second tallest in Britain, was unfortunately a casualty, as was the highest known *Acer macrophyllum*. Paths have recently been cleared so that these great trees, and others, can be seen to advantage.

The remainder of the garden dates from 1960 and was planned at that time by Percy Cane, a well-known London landscape architect. It lies to the south-west of the house and is protected from the Border winds at the top end by a curved wall. From a turret in it, there is a spectacular view of the garden, and an overview of the Teviot winding through the Border countryside, which is, indeed, used as a 'backcloth' to the garden itself, leading the gaze to a stone landing-place on the Teviot and to the pastoral country beyond.

The lay-out of Percy Cane's original garden, contained within the hedge, was in parallel lines. It was felt that these straight lines were not compatible with the rolling parkland, dotted with mature trees, and the winding river. This particular part of the estate has a Capability Brown feel to it. The now curving herbaceous borders lead the eye down to the open country and are also more in keeping with the curve of the upper wall. Here, again, Mr Simmons, a horticultural artist with a fine eye for colour combinations, was meticulous in his use of suitable plants. For instance, at one side you will find two specimens of *Cotinus coggygria* 'Royal Purple' beside a newly planted golden rhus. These are matched on the other side with two more cotinus of the same form, but this time combined with *Populus candicans aurora*, the Ontario poplar, or balm of Gilead.

Other recent developments include a greenhouse containing fuchsias being grown for later replanting outside. There is also a nursery for seedlings. Over 70% of the plants in the herbaceous borders have been grown from seed.

The surroundings of the house have also recently been planted with clematis and roses, including a huge 'Kiftsgate' and 'Sympathy', while in the Red Border there are the floribundas *Rosa* 'Eyepaint', *R* 'Evelyn Fison' and *R* 'Europeana' amongst others.

In further borders there are splashes of colour created by fuchsias, skimmia, variegated holly, Hybrid Tea roses, hostas, heaths, pinks, jasmine, dianthus, blue hibiscus, and the subtly pink *Eupatorium purpureum*, Hemp agrimony. The berries of a spreading *Rubus tricolour* were colouring up in September.

One of the most important of the recent developments has been the creation of what was once a boggy area into a delightful water garden with a pond, three islands and four arched bridges, which lead the eye forward. The visitor might well be surprised at the clearness of the water. The explanation is simple. Mr

Simmons placed bales of straw at certain spots, his theory being that the straw abstracts nitrogen, so necessary for plant growth, and this in turn inhibits the growth of blanket-weed. It certainly is a successful method at Monteviot. Here you will find damp-loving plants such as *Gunnera manicata*, the Himalayan blue poppy (meconopsis), astilbes, *Polygonum campanulatum*, and really superb *Polygonum superbum*.

On the approach to the Water Garden, there is another 'picture'. The huge horizontal limb of an aged oak forms the top of the framework, while a *Populus alba* forms one of the sides and contrasts in colour and texture, the whole providing a view of the river. Because of the antiquity of the oak, another has been planted against eventualities.

Next to the Water Garden a wild garden is being created for snowdrops, daffodils, scillas, primulas, rhododendrons and woodland flowers.

There are all sorts of unexpected delights in this magnificent garden — pink and white colchicums nestling among the roots of a tree; the straight lines of a hedge softened by beds of golden spiraea and artemisia; a perennial geranium edging border and fungi, such as fly agaric and puff balls (once used apparently to stem nose-bleeds!), popping up in autumn.

Monteviot is one of the few important, large gardens in Scotland not only in outstanding condition but also creatively expanding.

PITMEDDEN

Owner: National Trust for Scotland

Turn off A92 Aberdeen to Ellon road on to B999.
Pitmedden is about 16 miles from Aberdeen

Daily all year from 0930 hours to sunset

It is probable that the Romans first cultivated gardens
laid out in geometrical patterns, the plots filled with
plants called 'herbals' because of their medicinal
properties. Their descendants the Italians developed
floral gardens similarly designed, notably the Villa
d'Este. They in due course were copied by the
Frenchman Le Nôtre, who designed the formal gardens
at Versailles. Previously he had laid out those at the
château of Vaux-le-Vicomte.

The distinguished Scottish architect Sir William Bruce
of Balcaskie, a Royalist, found it convenient during
Cromwell's reign to do business in Holland. In reality,
his travels were a cover for carrying messages to and
from Charles II, exiled in France. Sir William was
influenced by what he had seen at Vaux-le-Vicomte
when he laid out the formal gardens at Kinross House. It
is therefore likely that when his friend Sir Alexander
Seton decided to lay out his Great Garden at Pitmedden,
Vaux-le-Vicomte would have been one influence.
Another was undoubtedly the garden at the Palace of
Holyroodhouse, which Sir William rebuilt for Charles II.

When Alexander began work on his new garden on 2
May 1675—the event is commemorated on the lintel of
the doorway which provides the entrance to his
garden—he would have watched its progress from the
fortified tower-house that was his home. This was
replaced by an unfortified mansion which was badly
damaged by fire in 1818. The same blaze probably
destroyed the original garden plans. This mansion was
pulled down in 1860, to be replaced by the present
Victorian edifice.

In 1894 the estate was put on the market and bought
by a wealthy farmer, Alexander Keith, whose son Major
James Keith (a distinguished agriculturalist) gave
Pitmedden to the National Trust for Scotland, along
with an endowment, in 1952, the year before he died.

Between 1955 and 1974, George Barron, at that time the Trust's head gardener, with the support of the Trust's representatives in the North-East, Mr and Mrs William Marjoribanks, and advice from various experts, including the then Lady Burnett of Leys (the creator with her husband, Sir James, of the garden at Crathes), set about the restoration of the Great Garden, which had by now degenerated into a weedy vegetable patch. Barron replaced the original herbals, formerly enclosed in the parterres, with modern bedding plants, thus giving seasonal colour. Dr James Richardson, the Inspector of Ancient Monuments in Scotland of the day, based the designs of three of the parterres on those of Gordon for Holyroodhouse, devising the fourth as a tribute to Sir Alexander Seton. It is laid out in the form of his coat of arms.

The garden is on two levels, the eastern half on an excavated lower level, so that it could be viewed from above. A high retaining wall shielded the garden from the north-east winds. To the south and north were viewing terraces, of which only the north one survives. It is flanked by two two-storey pavilions, ogival in outline, with rib-vaulted lower rooms and upper summerhouses, the southern one now repanelled with wood from a demolished mansion.

Sir Alexander's fountain, recessed into the entrance stair, has been restored, as has the elegant fountain that forms the focal point of the great garden. Some of the stones for it were taken from master-mason Robert Mylne's fountain which formerly stood at Linlithgow Cross, where it was erected to commemorate the Restoration of Charles II. The sundial is surrounded by a pavement of pebbles, taken from the River Dee, which were split by a hammer and then laid flat side up — an ancient craft.

The main features of the garden, apart from the splendid herbaceous borders along the garden wall, and the trimmed yews buttressing the wall itself, are the four rectangular parterres lined by box-hedges — three miles of them — divided by grass paths. Of the three modelled after the Holyroodhouse designs, that in the south-east corner carries the reminder *tempus fugit*, with fleurs-de-lys at each corner and two star patterns with elongated perpendicular points, flanking a sundial wearing 24 facets. The other two Holyroodhouse parterres consist of balancing formal figure designs.

The parterre commemorating the garden's founder, Sir Alexander Seton, has as its centrepiece his coat of arms and his initials SAS and DML, those of his wife, Dame Margaret Lauder. Surrounding the crest are the mottoes *sustento sanguine siga* (with blood I bear the standard), and *merces haec certa laborum* (the sure reward of our labours), referring to the death of John Seton, the third laird, killed with the Royalists while fighting for Charles I at the Battle of the Brig o' Dee in 1639. Incidentally, it is his crest that provides the design for the weather-vanes topping the two pavilions.

The skilful maintenance needed for the upkeep of this remarkable garden is considerable. The three miles of box-hedges and the yew buttresses have to be trimmed to shape every year. The annual plants that provide the colour, 40 000 of them, are raised in frames and glasshouses and planted out each May. The garden is, of course, at its best in August and early September when the bedding is in spectacular bloom.

Restoration still continues, one of the most recent additions being a herbal garden, designed by Dr Richardson and planted in the upper garden.

POLLOK HOUSE, Glasgow

Owner: Glasgow District Council

Pollok Estate, Glasgow

All year round (except Christmas Day and New Year's Day)
from 1000 hours to 1700 hours

Pollok House, on the right bank of the White Cart River, was built for Sir John Maxwell, the second Baronet, in 1747. Ten years before, he had commissioned plans from William Adam, but Adam died a few months after building commenced. Between 1890 and 1907, Sir Rowand Anderson added the wings and designed the terracing with its two pavilions along the south front. The two lions were sculpted by Hew Lorimer in the 1940s.

The present house is the third dwelling to be put up on the estate. The first, a fortified castle, is said to have stood by the White Cart River. The second, the Laigh Castle, stood on the site of the present stable courtyard. The adjacent garden wall incorporates part of one of the towers. It was inhabited until the middle of the 16th century.

The lands were granted by David I to Walter, the High Steward, about 1124. Later they were acquired, first by Rolland de Mearns and then by the Maxwells of Caerlaverock, Dumfriesshire. One Sir John Maxwell fought at Otterburn (1388) and another fell at the Battle of Dryffe Sands (1593). The last Sir John died childless in 1865, and the estate passed to his nephew, William Stirling of Keir. In 1939 the owner, John Stirling Maxwell, entered into a conservation agreement on the estate. In 1965 another agreement transferred the administration of the house and garden to the Glasgow Local Authority.

The survival of the house with its gardens and parkland in the midst of a city like Glasgow, which experienced expansion and industrial growth throughout the 19th century, is of itself remarkable. Part of the estate was feued off in 1851, when the development of Pollokshields began. Further portions were disposed of in the 1860s and again in the 1890s. About

11 000 acres remain. In 1908, that gardening enthusiast Sir Herbert Maxwell observed: 'The park of Pollok is but a green oasis round which Glasgow and the neighbouring burghs have flowed like a dark and rapidly rising tide. Yet here on the terrace wall, within constant sound of steam hooters and whistles, steam hammers and pumps, you may see alpine flowers blooming as profusely and with colours as clear as they do on the loftiest solitudes on earth and in the purest atmosphere.'

The industrial noises have long since fallen silent and the Clean Air Act has ensured that the air remains relatively pure. Both house and grounds are now a much-enjoyed Glasgow asset.

The grounds and the gardens were largely the creation of Sir John Stirling Maxwell who in 1888, to celebrate his 21st birthday, planted the spectacular lime avenue to the north of the house. Throughout his life he planted many other trees and rhododendrons in the park. To the east and south of the house, Sir John designed parterres. Once there were also parterres on the lawn that slopes down to the river, but these are now grassed over. The bridge over the river was put up in 1757.

Since Glasgow has assumed responsibility for the 60 acres of garden, which run to the east of the house, much new work has been undertaken. The area to the north of the main walk along the outside wall of the demonstration garden is being redeveloped. A cottage garden is also being constructed at the south end of the main garden, just above the stable courtyard.

The demonstration garden contains a rose garden, a nursery for young trees and examples of paving and other garden crafts for amateur gardeners to copy.

To the north-east of the house, Barry Gasson's prize-winning gallery housing the Burrell Collection of pictures and a wide variety of *objets d'art* fits admirably into the contours of the park.

Pitmedden *parterres*

page 162

Younger Botanic Garden
pond and autumn colour

page 190

Royal Botanic Garden Edinburgh   *page 169*
Orchid and Cycad House in the 'Glasshouse Experience'

Logan Botanic Garden   *page 147*
Water Garden and red-hot pokers

PRIORWOOD, Melrose, Roxburghshire

Owner: The National Trust for Scotland

By Melrose Abbey on B6361

April, November and December (to 24) daily from 1000 hours to 1300 hours and 1400 hours to 1730 hours (closed Sundays)
May, June and October daily from 1000 hours to 1730 hours (Sunday 1330 hours to 1730 hours)
July, August and September daily from 1000 hours to 1800 hours (Sunday 1300 hours to 1730 hours)

Priorwood, originally Priorbank, a charming cottage built against the south boundary wall of Melrose Abbey grounds, dates from around 1820. A map of John Wood, dated 1826, shows the garden already under cultivation. In 1940, the garden became a commercial market garden and was run for some years as such; but by 1974 it was derelict. Two years later, Betina, Lady Thomson offered financial help to the National Trust for Scotland to enable it to create the first (and only) garden in Britain dedicated to the growing and demonstration of everlasting flowers and plants for dry-flower work. It has 200 plants which can be used in this way. The herbal garden has a wide variety of sweetsmelling 'simples'. The striking wrought-iron work in the long 18th-century wall along the street front is thought to be by Lutyens.

The garden, over six acres, was probably first cultivated by the monks after the Abbey was founded in 1136. Today, among other things, it contains *Helichrysum* 'Elmstead' and *splendidum*; artemesias, alliums, achillea, solidago and anaphalis, as well as the more unusual *Phlomis samia* and *Rheum palmatum*, which originated in China.

There is a demonstration hut where different drying methods are displayed and explanatory leaflets for the 'do-it-yourself' flower-drier are available. There is also a shop selling dried flower arrangements, single flowers, bouquets, posies and pot-pourri.

In 1986, the Trust also established an orchard with an Apple Walk illustrating the development of the apple in Britain since Roman times. The many unusual varieties growing here include 'Adam's Pearmain', 'Peasgood's Nonsuch', 'Oslin' (believed to be the original 'Pippin'),

'Cambusnethan Pippin', 'Pomme d'Api', 'Court Pendu Plat' and 'Lane's Prince Albert'. The variety 'Royal Russet' dates from at least 1597.

The wild garden is drift-planted with flowers and shrubs also useful for drying.

ROYAL BOTANIC GARDEN EDINBURGH

Owner: The Royal Botanic Garden (Trustees)

Inverleith Row, Edinburgh

November to February (except 25 December and 1 January)
from 1000 hours to 1600 hours daily
March to April and September to October from 1000 hours to
1800 hours daily
May to August from 1000 hours to 2000 hours daily

The three oldest Botanic Gardens in Britain are those at Oxford (1621), Edinburgh (1670) and London's Chelsea Physic Garden (1673). The original purpose of all three was to produce plants for medicinal uses. The Royal Botanic Garden at Edinburgh was set up by two eminent men, Andrew Balfour (1630–94) and Robert Sibbald (1641–1715). Sibbald became Royal Physician, Geographer and Natural Historian to Charles II, who commissioned his survey of the geography, archaeology and flora of Scotland, *Scotia Illustrata*, published in 1682.

The original garden was at St Anne's Yard, Holyrood and became too small within six years. It therefore moved in 1676 to a site adjoining Trinity Hospital, where part of Waverley Station now stands. Though it expanded on this site in 1684, by 1763 it had to move again, this time to a five-acre site at Leith Walk, which once again it outgrew. It moved to its present Inverleith site in 1820. There has been further expansion, particularly during the present century. The Specialist Gardens at Logan, Dawyck and Benmore have been incorporated and new buildings have been constructed at Inverleith. A history of the combined gardens, *4 Gardens in One*, by Deni Bown, is published by the Royal Botanic Garden Edinburgh. She writes: 'The Garden at Inverleith is nothing short of a miracle and this is no time more apparent than in spring, when the lengthening days and warmer weather stir plants from all over the world into flower and new growth. It is proof that nature, given a helping hand from the gardener, can triumph over adversity and that the most luxuriant garden can be created on a thoroughly unpromising site. The Edinburgh adversity takes the form of poor sandy soil and low rainfall—only 24 inches (609.6mm) on average—which makes it the driest and least fertile of all the four gardens.'

While the main purpose of the garden is taxonomy, botanical research dealing with the accurate identification of plants and their classification and distribution, the garden affords manifold delights to thousands of visitors every year.

This 'miracle', which now covers just under 67 acres, is divided into sections for the purposes of guiding round the visitor.

Entering by the East Gate (on Inverleith Row), and passing the Library and Herbarium—opened by Her Majesty the Queen in 1964—which houses material for research and is not open to the public, the visitor will come upon the 'Glasshouse Experience'; both the marvellous Temperate Palmhouse of the 1850s and the architecturally equally striking new range, opened in 1967, divided into five climatic zones. They are particularly popular in winter, when so much outside is 'hibernating'.

Past the glasshouses is the Alpine house and courtyard. Inside, pleiones, including the rare *P forrestii*, are featured: outside, *Clematis alpina subsp sibirica*, a large Siberian *Fritillaria pallidiflora, Daphne mezereum* and, in the retaining wall of the raised bed, *Synthyris stellata* flourish. Trough gardens are a feature of the courtyard.

The winter garden collection includes *Mahonia bealei, Lonicera standishii, Eranthis hyemalis, Hepatica transsilvanica* and a wide range of hellebores.

The sectioned demonstration garden has a considerable display of roses, a bed of hardy annuals and a Mediterranean Garden. The cryptogamic garden of non-flowering plants contains ferns, horsetails, mosses, liverworts, lichens and fungi, including the razor-strop fungus, *Piptoporus betulinus*, which grows only on birch.

The herbaceous border is dormant in winter, but comes into full bloom throughout the summer. In due time, there are geraniums, including *Geranium*

'Johnson's Blue' and *G pratense*; hostas, including *H undulata* and *H sieboldii*; ornamental poppies, including *Papaver orientale* 'Olympia', as well as, in high summer, lupins, campanulas, nepeta, delphiniums, phlox and, later, Michaelmas daisies and Japanese anemones.

There is a peat garden which hosts, among much else, the late-flowering *Primula vialii*, *Nomocharis* and *N pardanthina* with, as summer advances, the yellow Turk's-cap lily, *L pyrenaicum* and, from Japan, the stately *L auratum*. Of the 80-plus species of lily and their hybrids, particularly spectacular is *Cardiocrinum giganteum*, the huge Himalayan lily.

The heath garden is designed to provide colour throughout the seasons. The pond area, developed in the 1820s and now well-covered with *Nymphoides peltata* and fringed at the margin with the flowering fern *Osmunda regalis*, is supplied with colour by astilbes, double meadowsweet, *Filipendula ulmaria* 'Flore Pene', *F purpurea*, *Mimulus cardinalis* and the Japanese flag, *Iris ensata*.

For tree-lovers, there is an arboretum—the 'backbone of the garden in structural terms,' according to Deni Bown—and a woodland garden, where many of the 400 or so splendid rhododendrons are to be found.

Perhaps the most marvellous of all the many aspects of this Edinburgh 'miracle' is the world-famous rock garden, its huge boulders and grassy hillocks, with streamlets and pools, spreading over a considerable area. In spring, there are crocuses, scillas, muscari and chinodoxas, narcissus and primula (the garden has many rare primulas, including *P pruhoniciana*), erythroniums and trilliums; in summer, *Penstemon newberryi*, *Symphyandra armena*, the yellow *Verbascum dumulosum* and the intensely blue *Delphinium grandiflorum* and *D tatsienense*. In autumn, the collections of gentians and colchicums are particularly eye-catching.

The range of interests covered by the Royal Botanic Garden—it is, in Deni Bown's words, 'the only botanical institute in Great Britain that can claim to cover the entire spectrum of plant life in its research programme'—and the number of plants, shrubs and trees it contains are alike so impressive that, despite the magnificent settings of so many of the great Scottish gardens, this one—with sloping vistas of Edinburgh rising up dramatically from various viewpoints—is without serious comparison in Britain, except, perhaps, from Kew.

ST ANDREWS BOTANIC GARDEN, St Andrews, Fife

Owner: North-East Fife District Council Department of Recreation

Between The Canongate and the Lade Braes Walk

From 1000 hours to 1900 hours daily from May to September; 1000 hours to 1600 hours from April to October; Monday to Friday from 1000 hours to 1600 hours from November to March

The original St Andrews Botanic Garden, in which beds of plants arranged in order of families were laid out, was located in a quarter of an acre of a walled garden just south of St Mary's College, planned and executed in 1889 by Dr John Wilson. In 1960, the move took place to Bassagard ('farm of the priests'), with its entrance on The Canongate. The present garden covers 18 acres.

The western end contains large plantings of trees and shrubs, notably pines and various species of rowan (sorbus), laced by sheltered paths. To the east are rock and peat gardens, through which a stream falls to an ornamental lake, with mimulus, the monkey flower, at the water's edge. Here, a wide variety of meconopsis, rhododendron and primula abounds. The lake runs out into the Kinness Burn.

On higher ground, covering one-fifth of an acre, there are tropical and temperate glasshouses, designed for display as well as research. These have been upgraded since the District Council took over responsibility for the garden in 1987. The Cacti House has been relandscaped, and now has almost 250 varieties, including *Echinocactus grusonii*, Barrel cactus, and *Opuntia violacea grosselina* 'Flapjack'. A landscaped area is being developed to enable visitors to admire rare alpines from all over the world. There is also to be an orchid and cycad house, as well as a temperate house with landscaped fishponds and streams.

A demonstration garden is being constructed, in which many aspects of gardening by the amateur will be expounded, including such features as the patio garden and gardening for the disabled. Dates and times may be obtained from the Botanic Garden itself, or by ringing

0334 53722 (Department of Recreation, County Buildings, Cupar, Fife).

There is a charitable organization, 'Friends of the Botanic Garden', for whom special visits and lectures are arranged, and who can receive surplus seed.

Echinocactus grusonii

ST MARY'S PLEASANCE, Haddington

Owner: Haddington Garden Trust
Off A1 Edinburgh to Dunbar road
Daily throughout the year during daylight hours

The ancient, well-preserved and still charming town of
Haddington has as its oldest building the Abbey of St
Mary's, dating from the 14th century. The western part
was restored as the Parish Church in 1811. Major
restoration of the Transept and Crossing was completed
in 1973. It has from ancient times been known as
Lucerna Loudionae, 'The Lamp of Lothian', the title
taken by the Collegiate Trust that, amongst other
activities, looks after the Poldrate Mill and Carlyle
House. Across from the churchyard stands 17th century
Haddington House. The Walled Garden that lies
between the Abbey and House was given by the late
Duke of Hamilton to the newly established Haddington
Garden Trust 'to preserve the garden at Haddington
House and develop it as an old Scottish Garden.' The
high brick wall which encloses it is said to have been
built by French prisoners during the Napoleonic Wars.
The walls were probably originally clothed with espa-
liered fruit trees, including an apricot tree. (For
instance, in 1785 at nearby Lennoxlove, there was a large
apricot tree one hundred years old). The delightful little
Apple House has now been fully restored.

By the 17th century, British gardeners had left behind
the previous century's fascination with the knot garden
and become more open in their designs. Parterres, or
plots bounded by small clipped box hedges, often in
geometrical designs, resulted in a greater sense of
spaciousness. Though herbs, vegetables and flowers
were often still grown in the same garden there was an
increasing awareness of the beauty of flowers cultivated
for their own sake.

One of the charms of this predominantly herb garden
lies in its layout. The large central lawn is dotted with
specimen trees (not the originals) which would have
been grown in the 17th century. Here, you will find
among others *Morus nigra*, the common mulberry,
Liriodendron tulipifera, the Tulip tree, as its name

suggests, and *Acer negundo*, the Box elder, which was first cultivated in 1688 by Bishop Compton. Round the lawn are beds and borders containing every conceivable type of herb with information about its individual properties.

The main entrance is from Sidegate and leads directly to the Sunken Garden beside Haddington House itself. Here, the box-edged parterre, with at each corner a large quern, is banked round the four sides of the rectangle. Two opposite banks are planted with at the top *Lavandula spica, the 'oyle to perfume linnen, apparrell, gloves . . . The dryed flowers dry up the moisture of a cold braine,' according to Parkinson in 1629. Beneath the lavender, Ruta graveolens*, or Garden rue, carries the notice, 'Boyled and kept in pickle and eaten, quicketh the sight' (Gerard 1597). This in turn is fronted by a border of *Hyssopus officinalis* which in a 'decoction' combined with fig leaves and 'gargled in the mouth and throat, ripeneth and breaketh the tumours and impostumes of the mouth and throat . . . coming by cold rheumes.' (Gerard 1597). Another bank hosts *Vinca major*, while at the opposite end, pink *Teucrium chamaedrys*, germander, flourishes and, according to Parkinson in 1629, was useful for strewing about the house.

Other beds around the walls contain a wide variety of old-fashioned herbs and information as to their uses. Anyone suffering from almost any ailment could find a cure here. Not all herbs, however, are beneficial. For instance, *Santolina chamaecyparissus*, as its common name 'Sea wormwood' would suggest, is 'not used in phisicks.' There is a magnificent *Laburnum alpinum* Walk but laburnum is not recommended as it causes vomiting, 'which it will do very strongly.' Those suspecting an iminent outbreak of plague could do no better than employ the Sweet woodruff, *Asperula odorata*!

There are, of course, all kinds of other plants, too numerous to be listed, which are in the enthusiastic care of John Grieve. This is certainly a garden of great charm and fascination.

SCONE PALACE

Owner: The Earl of Mansfield

2 miles north of Perth on A93 Perth to Blairgowrie road

Monday to Saturday 0930 hours to 1700 hours; Sundays 1300 hours (July and August 1000 hours) to 1700 hours all year round

Scone Palace was originally a Bishop's Palace and not a royal one. At the Abbey of Scone (destroyed by a mob incited by John Knox in 1559), many of the early Scottish kings were crowned. Fictionally, Shakespeare's Macbeth bled to death at Scone and Malcolm, his successor, was crowned there. The last Scottish king to be crowned at Scone was John de Balliol. They were crowned on the Stone of Destiny, possibly brought from Dunstaffanage in AD838, and kept at Scone for 500 years until taken south to Westminster Abbey by Edward I, 'the Hammer of the Scots'.

The palace escaped the Knox-inspired sacking. It had been built by the Earls of Gowrie, one of whom was involved in the Gowrie Conspiracy at Perth against James VI. A Murray, an antecedent of the present Earl of Mansfield, 'happened to be passing' at the time of the king's greatest need and effected his rescue, as a result of which the family was rewarded with the present lands.

Between 1802 and 1808, the 3rd Earl of Mansfield had the architect, William Atkinson, restyle the palace in what has come to be known as 'Walter Scott Gothic'. Parkland fronting two miles of the River Tay surrounds it.

For garden-lovers, the stately pinetum will be the main attraction. It was laid out in 1848, although its most famous ornament is the enormous Douglas Fir, *Pseudotsuga menziesii*, sent as seed from America in 1827 by David Douglas, the famous collector, who was born on the estate and at one time worked for the palace as an undergardener. The pinetum also contains Giant Sequoia Redwoods and Sitka Spruce, as well as other Douglas Firs, some over 150 feet high.

The family chapel and burial place of the Mansfields on the adjacent Moot Hill, an artificial mound on which Scotland's chieftains once swore their oaths of loyalty to newly crowned kings, is backed by an impressive cluster of Giant Cedars of Lebanon, *Cedrus libani*.

To the south of the palace is a small garden with a variety of rhododendrons and azaleas, the few surviving stones of the Abbey and paths said once to lead to the 'Monks' Playgreen' and the 'Friars' Den'. There is also in season a splendid 'field of daffodils', and a pergola over which in early summer laburnums drip. Peacocks shriek and besport themselves on the wide lawns around the palace.

SIR DOUGLAS BADER GARDEN for the DISABLED, Cupar

Owner: N E Fife District Council

Left off A91 Stirling to St Andrews road at Balgarvie Road just short of Cupar town centre and almost immediately left up narrow road

Daily throughout the year

The Sir Douglas Bader Garden for the Disabled, opened by him in 1982 and whose initials are incorporated in the charming wrought-iron gates, by its very nature is small, the total area comprising 1740 square metres, of which quite a major portion is at the moment laid out in grass. With its raised beds and broad paved paths, it is reminiscent of the same type of garden laid out by the Royal Horticultural Society at Wisley, Surrey. But, what an enlightened creation for any District Council to have conceived and one which should be emulated!

On entering the garden, there is a considerable paved area which contains sheltered seating (the entire garden is sheltered), a fountain and pool, an aviary (presumably in summer it will contain a variety of birds) and a raised circular block marked out in squares for playing outdoor draughts. Raised beds are essential for the disabled. Here, they contain prostrate junipers and other conifers amongst much else: a lovely ceanothus, lavender, gentians and thymes. Colour is supplied by plots and beds of scarlet salvia, variegated dwarf pelargoniums and calceolaria, as well as a skilful choice of shrubs and small trees. In other words, visitors can touch and feel and look at the plants at a convenient level.

The designers have been careful to use several differently textured materials to add variety. Apart from the stonework, the fences are of brick and wood, both of solid and 'hit and miss' construction. There is also a stout wooden pergola. The paved paths lead the visitor towards plots filled with shrubs such as acers, forsythia, *Cotinus coggygria*, harmonising with *Berberis* 'Atro-purpurea', a willow, *Salix lanata*, and for fun, two specimens of *Corylus avellana contorta*, or 'corkscrew hazel', otherwise known to Scots as 'Harry Lauder's Walking Stick'.

This is a garden which keeps up with the times. When work was first started on it, a tree was planted to commemorate the Royal Wedding on 29 July 1981; a golden yellow *Gleditsia triacanthos* 'Sunburst', or honey locust, commemorated its first anniversary and as recently as this year, yet another tree was planted to commemorate the 50th Anniversary of the D-Day landings on 6 June 1944.

Plans are afoot to continue landscaping; to renew existing borders and beds and to plant many more roses back from the walking areas in order that injuries can be avoided. For those whose sight is impaired, raised edging round the paths acts as a guideline. Every consideration has been given here to the disabled. For instance, seats are placed conveniently throughout the garden. It is emphasised that this is not a 'show' garden but a working one for community involvement, interest and enjoyment — wheelchair dancing, talks and various classes have either taken place, or are envisaged.

Dare one perhaps take the liberty of suggesting that to increase the garden's fragrance, beds of the sweet-smelling pinks, *Dianthus caryophyllis* and *superbus* might be planted, along with the more highly perfumed lilies, nicotiana and night-scented stock? These would add additional scent to a garden the management of which does not stand still, but is always looking forward to the future.

STONEFIELD CASTLE HOTEL

Owner: Peter Ross

2 miles from Tarbert on A83 Glasgow to Campbeltown road

Daily throughout the year

Stonefield Castle (originally called Barmore) was built in 1837 by Sir W H Playfair for the Campbell family on the western shore of Loch Fyne, two miles north of Tarbert. In the Scottish Baronial style, it has for some years been an hotel. Set in about 50 acres of woodland gardens, which slope down on one side to the loch-shores and on the other up the hill, it contains some of the finest examples of Himalayan rhododendrons, many of them the older species (some over 100 years old) introduced by Sir Joseph Hooker (son of the first Professor of Botany at Glasgow University) and illustrated in his book *The Rhododendrons of the Sikkim Himalaya*.

Like so many fine west-coast gardens in Scotland, Stonefield enjoys a clement climate, a considerable rainfall and the acid soil in which rhododendrons flourish. Unlike their natural habitat in Sikkim or Bhutan, they are not grown in Scotland at an altitude of some 9000 to 12000 feet! Naturally vigorous species such as *R arboreum, campanulatum, cinnabarinum, falconeri, grande, campylocarpum* and *triflorum*, which grow to a great height in the Himalayas, achieve much the same size in Stonefield and some are even regenerating themselves naturally throughout the grounds. Dr Campbell Oronsay, a relative of the Stonefield Campbells, accompanied Hooker on his expeditions and, like so many others, sent back seed to Scotland and to Stonefield.

Besides being noted for its rhododendron collection, Stonefield is host to many other exotic shrubs including the Chilean *Philesia buxifolia* with its bell-shaped, waxy flowers, which has to be strictly controlled, otherwise its robust behaviour would cause it to take over. *Fuchsia excorticata* from New Zealand, incredibly, is now 15 feet high and almost 20 feet across, while the brilliant red young foliage of *Pieris* 'Forrestii' (a George Forrest find) lives up to its name. Today, it is 18 feet high and is indeed almost a forest, considerably outsizing, it seems, a similar form of much lesser stature at Bodnant. There is also a fine collection of magnolias. In autumn, like so many other such gardens, the colour is particularly fine.

Pieris 'FORRESTII'

STRONE, Cairndow, Argyll

Owner: John Noble

At the head of Loch Fyne on A83 Inveraray to Arrochar road

April to September daily during the hours of daylight

This woodland garden of 15 acres beside the River Kinglas is justly famous for its huge conifers and extensive collection of unusual rhododendrons. The conifers were planted over a century ago by the Callenders, who took over the land from the Campbells of Ardkinglas. In the pinetum there is, for example, a Giant Fir, *Abies grandis*, planted in 1875, now over 208 feet high, and the tallest tree in Great Britain. There is also a massive *Abies alba* whose girth is over 29 feet. Rivalling these trees in height are some Sawara cypresses, *Chamaecyparis pisifera* 'Squarrosa'. There are also fine examples of *Araucaria araucana*, *Chamaecyparis obtusa*, the Hinoki cypress, *Fitzroya cupressoides* (the tallest of its kind in Britain), *Larix decidua*, *Picea abies*, *P orientalis*, *P polita*, *Thuya plicata*, *Tsuga heterophylla* and *T mertensiana*.

The estate was bought by Sir Andrew Noble in 1905. His son and grandson, Sir John and Michael Noble respectively, began planting rhododendrons around 1930. To start them off, Lord Aberconway sent two railtrucks of plants from Bodnant. A large consignment of azaleas was bought in Belgium at one shilling (5 pence) per plant. There were also later gifts from, and exchanges with, such other famous gardeners as Sir George Campbell of Succoth (and his son, Sir Ilay), Sir Eric Savill of Windsor and Sir James Horlick of Gigha, among others.

The sandy loam soil, the Gulf Stream's mild influence and heavy rainfall at the head of Loch Fyne (80–100 inches per annum) favour ericaceous plants, especially rhododendrons.

As Laird of Strone, Michael Noble, Secretary of State for Scotland from 1958 to 1965, became greatly enthusiastic about hybridizing rhododendrons, seeking to produce a well-shaped bush or tree with regular flowering, scent if possible, and resistance to frost and hail. The plants he used most frequently and with considerable success were *griffithianum, elliotti, haematodes* and *maddenii*. Perhaps rather less successfully, he also used *johnstoneanum, brumanicum* and *lindleyi*. As a result of his work, there is now a splendid collection of superb red hybrids from March to mid-June, and an interesting selection of pinks, whites and creams in addition.

Spectacular big-leaved specimens include two large *falconeri* and two *arizelum K W 20922*. There are also some outstanding crosses of *wardii* with *wardii*.

Upstream from the pinetum, the 'New Garden' contains cherries, magnolias, camellias, eucalyptus, sorbus and azaleas, as well as the more unusual embothrium. All the azaleas are Lord Glenkinglas's own hybrids. In spring, hosts of daffodils and bluebells add their special charm.

It is encouraging to find that with natural regeneration, young seedling beeches, oaks, sycamores and conifers are springing up among the ancient trees, as well as on the carpets of brilliant green sphagnum moss. If you are lucky, as we were, you may even see a shy red squirrel (rare now in Scotland, thanks to attack by their militant grey brothers) scrambling up the gnarled barks.

The best time to visit this garden is from mid-April to mid-June, when the daffodils and the wild hyacinths are in bloom, and the leaves of the hardwood trees are alight with a translucent green.

THREAVE SCHOOL of GARDENING, Castle Douglas

Owner: The National Trust for Scotland

1 mile from Castle Douglas on A75

Garden, all year round to dusk; walled garden and glasshouses, all year from 0900 hours to 1700 hours; visitor centre 1 April to 31 October, from 0900 hours to 1730 hours; restaurant from 1000 hours to 1700 hours

Threave (originally Trieffe) was the name of the Black Douglas's castle built in the 12th century on the River Dee, within the bounds of the present estate. In 1867, a Liverpool business man, William Gordon, had the Glasgow firm of architects, Peddie and Kinnear, build for him a Baronial-style house. Three generations of Gordons lived in it, the third consisting of two unmarried brothers. Major Colin Gordon (a former Guards officer like his brother) died in 1942, Major Alan in 1957. In 1948, Major Alan approached the Trust to take over Threave on his death, which they did.

The estate consists of four main farms, three smaller holdings and 150 acres of woodland. The house itself stands in 60 acres of parkland, much of it now developed by the Trust as a garden. There is also a wildfowl refuge on 301 acres, purchased later.

Although the main aim at Threave since it took in its first students in October 1960 was, and still is, to train the gardeners of the future, so many and varied are the requirements of such training that the gardens have now developed into a colourful and interesting experience for visitors, whose numbers increase yearly.

Behind the visitor centre and restaurant is the rose garden, where old-fashioned and shrub roses predominate in the large informal beds. In this area there is a Weeping ash, *Fraxinus excelsior pendula*, transplanted to its present site in 1963, when 80 years old—no easy feat. There is also a large example of *Rosa filipes* and fine specimens of *Viburnum x bodnantense* flowering from November to April. In late summer, colour is provided by flaming spiky lavatera. Modern bedding roses adorn the Longwood Steps built in 1976 to mark the link, formed ten years earlier, whereby students are exchanged every year between Threave and the Long-wood Gardeners in the USA.

Just below the rose garden is the woodland garden, housing plants that prefer shade and moisture, as well as bulbs and hybrid rhododendrons. Interesting trees include a 40-foot-high metasequoia and a 'Chilean Fire Bush', *Embothrium coccineum*.

At the lower end of the woodland garden is the small heath garden. The winter border houses plants with coloured stems like the Golden willow, *Salix britzensis*, and flowering shrubs such as *Garrya elliptica, Viburnum bodnantense* and hamamelis. The paved patio area nearby was laid out as a student project in 1972.

The one-acre walled garden, approached from the patio, was first laid out in 1870 to provide fruit and vegetables for the house. The greenhouses date from 1960. There is a herb garden and a trough garden. Several herbaceous borders also add their bright colours. Behind the walled garden is the nursery, where the raising of a variety of hedging plants is a regular feature.

Outside the walled garden, the peat garden, sheltered by trees on two sides, houses dwarf rhododendrons, vaccinium, gaultheria, primula, meconopsis, gentians, dwarf primula (of particular interest are the *Primula vialii*, the 'red-hot poker' form), and among other lovers of moist, acid soil, *Gentiana asclepidaea*. The locally cut peat blocks last from eight to ten years. Nearby is a waterfall and pond and some newly raised varieties of pernettya.

The rock garden, the Trust says, 'is not a rock garden for the connoisseur, but rather one that is designed to be colourful over as long a period as possible, within the limitations of climate and the naturally heavy soil'.

A small formal garden, on the site of a previous vegetable garden, was constructed by students in 1988–9. Six types of such arrangements are included: a knot garden; a rose and clematis garden; raised beds; a silver and gold area; a topiary and a parterre.

A park and a grass collection lie between it and a

'secret garden', entered through a laburnum arch. It contains a sunken garden, a Japanese garden lantern and some fine trees, including a golden Scots pine, *Pinus sylvestris* 'Aurora' and an *Acer palmatum* 'Osakazuki'. There is also a dwarf conifer plantation beyond the 'secret garden'.

A large arboretum begun in 1965 takes in a hill face reaching round behind Threave House. It includes a collection of hollies.

Other delights are a heather garden with a spectacular view over the Galloway hills, and an orchard containing more than 20 varieties of Scottish pears and such old Scottish apples as 'Tower of Glamis', 'East Lothian Seedling' and 'Cambusnethan Pippin'.

The drive, though normally seen by visitors only from their cars, also has interesting plants. Opposite the car park is a cherry and crab apple collection, while down by the lodge there are some of the largest trees in the garden. On either side of the gate, two specimens of young 'Dawyck' beech flourish.

A walk along the path of the former railway line, which runs through the estate, is a rewarding experience, lined as it is with wild flowers; so, too, is a visit to the spectator hides in the wildfowl range along two miles of the River Dee.

Despite the fact that Threave Gardens are, for the most part, of comparatively recent layout, already they offer the visitor an exceptionally wide range of horticultural delights. The visitor centre is exceedingly well stocked with gardening books.

TOROSAY CASTLE, Isle of Mull

Owner: Mr Christopher James

By Craignure

Daily in the summer from 0900 hours to 1900 hours

The gardens of Torosay Castle, the most spectacular on the island, now cover 11 acres and gain an added dimension by being set in the midst of wild and magnificent Highland scenery. The name 'Torosay' derives from the Gaelic *torr rasach*, 'hill of the shrubs'. The land was originally owned by the Dukes of Argyll, who sold it in the 1820s to the Macquarries of Ulva, who in turn disposed of it to Colonel Campbell of Possil (Possil was then a village on the edge of Glasgow). During the 1850s, the small Georgian house that went with the land was demolished and the present mansion completed in 1858 by the architect David Bryce. Torosay came into the Guthrie family in 1865. In 1897 it was left to Walter Murray Guthrie (great-grandfather of the present owner). A grassy slope and a few Monkey Puzzle trees alone separated the house from the walled garden.

About the turn of the century, Walter Murray Guthrie brought in an expert, who devised a series of descending Italianate terraces to link the house and the walled garden. These boast splendid herbaceous borders. He also devised the Statue Walk, for which a series of 19 statues by Antonio Bonazza (1698–1765) from a derelict garden near Padua were shipped from Genoa to Glasgow and then taken by puffer to Mull. They are now said to comprise the finest collection of their kind outside Italy. The statues, representing work-a-day figures (with the exception of a mysterious lady in a cloak), stand amidst a rich display of rhododendrons, azaleas and fuchsias.

The Fountain Terrace, balustered and flanked by two gazebos, has lying below it two large, crouching statues giving their name to the Lion Terrace. The beasts are called 'Smiler' and 'Growler'.

The water garden (on the edge of which tall, red Candelabra primulas, desfontainea and euphorbia flourish, encouraged by the warmth of the Gulf Stream), was laid out by Murray Guthrie and restored by his son-in-law, the late Colonel Miller, during the 1960s. The Colonel was also responsible for the creation of the

Japanese garden, an ensemble of gravel, rocks and water, making use of the Japanese idea of 'borrowed landscape', which frames the magnificent view across the water to the seat of the Macleans, Duart Castle. A red Japanese bridge, spanning the lily-pond, forms the focal point of this garden. There is here, as well, a selection of acers and pine trees, each tactically placed for the maximum effect. To the surprise of some visitors, perhaps, Torosay contains a magnificent collection of deciduous trees, such as beeches, oaks and chestnuts, more often found in the Lowlands.

The rock garden nearby was the only part of the garden maintained during World War II, although it, too, became overgrown after the death in 1945 of the great-grandmother of the present owner, Mr Guthrie-James. The restoration of this, and so much else, has been lovingly carried out by Jaquetta James, his mother. Paths with rock plants weave their way around a central pool.

Once, in the 1930s, six full-time gardeners tended Torosay. Now, in the care of Christopher James, a much smaller force keeps the gardens in excellent trim for the delectation of those visitors who, since the construction of Craignure Pier in 1964, have been able to make a day excursion to Torosay from Oban and beyond.

Amongst the famous visitors to the castle have been Sir Winston Churchill (the Churchills were related to the Guthrie-James family), reputed to have brought down his first stag nearby. The late Earl Mountbatten's father, Vice-Admiral Prince Louis of Battenburg, was also a frequent visitor, as was King George of Greece.

YOUNGER BOTANIC GARDEN, Benmore

Owner: Royal Botanic Garden Edinburgh

On A815, 7 miles north of Dunoon, Argyll

15 March to 31 October daily from 1000 hours to 1800 hours. Other times by special arrangement

Benmore, as the Younger Botanic Garden is more usually known, is situated on the Cowal Peninsula, in the valleys of the River Eachaig and its tributary the Massan, between the Holy Loch and Loch Eck. When the estate on which the gardens now stand was a deer-hunting ground of the Dukes of Argyll, it was known as Inisninruisg, 'Vale of the Fleeces'. It was only comparatively recently that it became known as Benmore, after the mountain Beinn Mhor, which dominates the western shore of Loch Eck. Here, the annual rainfall is comparatively heavy (from 80–120 inches per annum), much of it experienced in the late autumn and early winter months. Benmore therefore provides almost ideal growing conditions for rhododendrons, conifers, and plants from areas of high rainfall, like the foothills of the Himalayas.

The first planting laird was Ross Wilson, who in 1820 began establishing Scots pine, Norwegian spruce and European larch, among other trees, on the lower slopes of the hill, A' Chruach. These conifers were the first to be grown in the Cowal peninsula.

Piers Patrick acquired the estate in 1862. He built the tower that is now part of Benmore House, and in 1863 had the foresight to plant an avenue of giant redwoods, *Sequoiadendron giganteum*, whose magnificent stature still dominates the approach to the gardens.

A Greenock sugar refiner, James Duncan, became the estate owner in 1863, adding his estates of Kilmun and Bernice to it to make his land in all extend to over 11 000 acres. Between 1871 and 1883 he planted no fewer than 6 480 000 trees on hitherto bare hills! In 1874 he also built on the main portion of Benmore House to the original tower. Among his other achievements were the construction of a sugar mill and an art gallery, both no longer standing, and, in 1875, the placing of the clock (still working) in the steading tower. His greenhouse were blown down during a storm in the 1930s, while hi. great conservatory survived only to succumb to the ferocious gale that struck the west of Scotland in January 1968. Duncan also experimented with iron-smelting at the head of Puck's Glen and silver-mining at Blairmore. Clearly, he was a lively-minded and innovative laird.

The estate changed hands again in 1889, when it was purchased by Henry J Younger, a member of the well-known Edinburgh brewing concern. He, and later his eldest son, Henry George, continued to plant trees, shrubs and perennial ornamental plants.

Around 1913, Henry George Younger established an area of exotic shrubs south of the avenue. It was he who, when selling the Bernice part of the policies in 1925, decided to gift the Benmore estate to the nation, with the intention that it should become a national demonstration centre for forestry and arboriculture.

As it happened, at about the same time, some of the seeds and plants sent back from Western China by George Forrest were thought by Sir Isaac Bayley Balfour, the Regius Keeper of the Botanic Garden at Edinburgh, to have a better chance of survival on a west-coast site rather than in the colder climate of Scotland's east coast. Preliminary plantings had already begun at nearby Glenbranter. On the acquisition of Benmore, most of these were transferred to the new estate, though some rhododendrons were left and now form part of the Forestry Commission's 'Harry Lauder Trail' (named after the Scots comedian famous in the first half of the 20th century).

Balfour's successor, Sir William Wright Smith, in 1925 established Benmore as the Royal Botanic Garden's first outstation. He is commemorated by the Wright Memorial Shelter at the viewing station on Benmore Hill, at the garden's highest point (450 feet above sea level). In 1929, the management of the garden passed from the Forestry Commission to the Royal Botanic Garden, although ownership was not transferred until 1975.

Wartime overgrowing, especially by the ubiquitous and dreaded rhododendron, *ponticum*, took some *ears to bring back under control, but successive keepers have further developed the garden, which is now visited by 45 000 people every year.

Following the storm of 1968, when hurricane winds of 130mph hit the west coast and did enormous damage, the clearance process made way for fresh planting. In 1975, 450 rhododendrons and 200 conifers were transferred to Benmore from Edinburgh. Throughout the 1980s, further extensive planting of conifers took place, together with the establishing of hundreds more rhododendrons. The Bhutanese Glade, given over to vegetation found in the Himalayan foothills of Bhutan, was established in 1989 at the western end of Glen Massan and, in 1990, major additional hybrid rhododendron collections were established. Here will be found areas dominated by such species as *Pinus wallichiana, Larix griffithiana* and *Abies densa*.

In spring, the avenue from the reception area to the River Eachaig, which runs through the garden from Loch Eck on its way to the Holy Loch, is carpeted with daffodils. In June, the scarlet *Rhododendron griersonianum* is in full flower and, as might be expected, the garden is ablaze with colour in the autumn. The Eachaig Arboretum has fine specimens of *Rhododendron fulvum, R fulgensia* and *R falconeri*. There are also some exceptional rugged-barked Douglas firs and an *Abies nordmanniana* over 152 feet in height.

Patrick's Pond has a fountain statue of 1860 and a wooden bridge leading to an island where there is a range of azaleas and Japanese maples. The stream through the gully nurtures herbaceous plants, including *Polygonum campanulatum*, early-flowering *Rhododendron dauricum* and *R mucronatum* as well as *R ferrugineum*.

The formal garden, once a traditional walled garden with large conservatories at each side, was redesigned in the late 1960s. The enormous range of cypress varieties, *Chamaecyparis lawsoniana,* which lines the eastern and southern walls is an unforgettable sight, reminding the visitor that the variety of shades of green seems endless. Former Regius Keepers of the Royal

Botanic Garden Edinburgh are commemorated: Si. Isaac Bayley Balfour with the rustic Puck's Hut, and Harold Fletcher with an armillary sphere.

Numerous walks to viewpoints can be taken through the hilly woodland, depending on energy and available time. One such leads to the highest point in the garden (yellow route), where there is a spectacular view of Strath Eck from the top of Benmore.

For many, the Rhododendron Walk (blue route), crossing the lower slopes of Benmore, may prove even more rewarding. On the way will be seen, in season, the spectacular colour of the azalea lawn; a new collection of *Rhododendron yakushimanum* hybrids; magnolias, including a lovely *campbellii*; the Chilean lantern bush, *Crinodendron hookerianum*, and the splendid rhododendrons — *cinnabarinum, campanulatum* and such large examples of the species as *praestans* and *sinogrande*.

In such a brief summary as this, it is quite impossible to mention more than a few of the innumerable trees, shrubs and flowers which this large, beautifully kept specialist and scenic garden contains. Not the least of its pleasures is the clear way in which the names of its fascinating vegetative inhabitants are labelled.

Select Bibliography

Buxbaum, Tim, *Scottish Garden Building: from Food to Folly*, Mainstream Publishing, Edinburgh, 1989

Cox, E H M, *A History of Gardening in Scotland*, Chatto and Windus, London, 1935

Haldane, E S, *Scots Gardens in Old Times (1200–1800)*, Alexander Maclehose, London, 1934

Hussey, C, 'The Work of Sir Robert Lorimer', *Country Life*, London, 1931

Kingdon Ward, Frank, *Plant Hunting on the Edge of the World*, Gollancz, London, 1930

Mackenzie, Osgood, *A Hundred Years in the Highlands*, 1921

MacLeod, Dawn, *The Gardener's Scotland*, William Blackwood, Edinburgh, 1977; *Down to Earth Women*, William Blackwood, Edinburgh, 1982; *Oasis of the North: A Highland Garden*, Melven Press, Perth, 1980

Maxwell, Sir Herbert, *Scottish Gardens: a retrospective selection of all types*, Edward Arnold, London, 1911

Reid, John (fl. 1620), *The Scots Gard'ner, published for the climate of Scotland*, Mainstream, Edinburgh, 1988

Truscott, James, *Private Gardens of Scotland*, Weidenfeld and Nicolson, London, 1988

Verney, Peter, *The Gardens of Scotland*, Batsford, London, 1976

The Royal Botanic Garden Edinburgh Book of the Scottish Garden, Mowbray House Publishing, Edinburgh, 1989

4 Gardens in One, The Royal Botanic Garden Edinburgh, text by Deni Bown, HMSO, Edinburgh, 1992

The Gardens of Scotland, edited by G Allan Little, Spurbooks, in association with Scotland's Gardens scheme, Edinburgh, 1981

The Gardens of Scotland, Scotland's Garden Scheme, Edinburgh, 1993